and the material presented in the pages which follow will likely trigger new questions not answered here.

Remember, your learning curve is not a destination, but a journey. As questions arise we encourage you call or write to us, because your continued growth and success as a professional Notary Signing Agent professional does not depend on having all the right answers, but in asking the right questions.

# NSA Q&A

Real-world
answers to the
Notary Signing Agent's
most-asked
questions

Published by:

**National Notary Association Press**
9350 De Soto Ave., P.O. Box 2402
Chatsworth, CA 91313-2402
Telephone: (818) 739-4000
FAX: (818) 700-0920
E-mail: nna@NationalNotary.org

The information in this *NSA Q&A* is correct and current at time
of publication, although new laws, regulations and rulings may
subsequently affect the validity of certain sections. This information
is provided to aid comprehension of state Notary Public requirements
and should not be construed as legal advice. Please consult an
attorney for inquiries relating to legal matters.

Second Edition

ISBN No. 1-59767-003-0
IL.C. Control Number: 2005924714

# Introduction

*"The key to wisdom is knowing all the right questions".*
*— John A. Simone, Jr.*

*"The wise man doesn't give the right answers, he poses the right questions".* *— Claude Levi-Strauss*

****

As with any new endeavor you take on, there is a learning curve. In the Notary Signing Agent vocation, it is no different. You have much to learn, and no doubt you have many questions. Some of those questions might include:

- How do I become a Notary Public and notarize documents legally?

- How do I most effectively market my Notary Signing Agent services?

- How do I negotiate contracts and set fees?

- How can I manage accounts so that I am paid for the services I perform?

- How does the mortgage finance industry work?

- How can I become familiar with real property terms and documents?

- How can I provide excellent customer service both to borrowers and clients?

- How can I manage my time and schedule?

- How do I keep records of my business activity?

- How do I report my Notary Signing Agent income on my tax forms?

It always helps to have a trusted guide to help navigate the bends in the road. That's where *NSA Q&A* comes in. Since establishing the Notary Signing Agent Section in 2002, the National Notary Association has received hundreds of questions from Notaries eager to investigate this burgeoning new vocation at Notary Signing Agent seminars, in calls fielded by staff on the Notary Signing Agent Hotline and at annual NNA Conferences.

*NSA Q&A* is a compilation of answers to many of these common questions arranged under the following chapters:

1. **Starting Out** — Questions about becoming a Notary Signing Agent and setting up your business.

2. **Preparing for the Signing** — Questions about real estate terminology, mortgage loans and loan documents and managing appointment logistics.

3. **Carrying Out the Signing** — Questions that arise in the context of loan signings, such as how to best identify an elderly woman without a driver's license, what to include in a journal entry and innumerable "What do I do when...?" questions.

4. **Closing Out the Signing** — Questions on how to wrap up assignments, keep business records, manage collections and file taxes.

Both new and experienced Notary Signing Agents alike will benefit from the wealth of information provided in *NSA Q&A*,

Table of
Contents

1

# Starting Out

## QUALIFICATIONS AND CREDENTIALS

**Besides being a Notary Public, are there any additional credentials I must obtain to conduct home loan signings?**

In most states, no additional professional licenses are required. There are a handful of states that require Notaries who conduct a real estate closing to be licensed as an escrow or title insurance producer. States with an additional license requirement include Indiana, Maryland and Virginia.

The rationale for why unlicensed Notaries are not authorized to perform a loan signing in these states is that there would be a loss of protection to the consumer if an unrecoverable error was made. As is the case with "attorney-only" states (see below), often there is a court case which sets a legal precedent or is the impetus for enactment of a law requiring licensure.

Although the process varies by state, candidates for escrow or title insurance licensee must satisfy the application, character, examination and education requirements specified under law or administrative rule. In addition, some states require licensees to receive an appointment by an insurance carrier, to be bonded and to carry errors and omissions insurance. All of the above mentioned states require licensees to complete mandatory continuing education courses on a yearly or biennial basis.

It is best to check with your state's insurance regulating agency to determine if you must earn an escrow or title insurance license.

**I have heard about the "attorney-only" states, but I don't know what this means or whether I live in one.**

"Attorney-only" states allow only attorneys to conduct real estate settlements and prosecute for the unauthorized practice of law any nonattorneys providing closing services, unless under an attorney's direct supervision. The states that can be classified as attorney-only states are: Delaware, Georgia, Massachusetts, South Carolina, Vermont and West Virginia.

As is common in most attorney-only states, there is not a specific statute prohibiting nonattorneys from conducting settlements that one can point to. Rather, case law is the deciding legal precedent.

In Delaware, for example, this precedent is the 2000 Delaware Supreme Court opinion *In Re: Mid-Atlantic Settlement Services*. In this lengthy ruling, the Supreme Court concluded:

1. A Delaware attorney is required to conduct a closing of a sale of Delaware real property.

2. A Delaware attorney is required to conduct a closing of a refinance loan secured by Delaware real property.

3. A Delaware attorney is required to be involved in a direct or supervisory capacity in drafting or reviewing all documents affecting transfer of title to Delaware real property or in refinance transactions in Delaware, with the exception of home equity loans. In the case of home equity loans, a lender, but not a Notary Signing Agent, may perform closing services.

4. A Delaware attorney "is necessary in evaluating the legal rights and obligations of the parties, representing the buyer in examining the title and removing exceptions to the title, supervising the disbursement of funds, and responding to questions concerning the legal effect of documents" (emphasis added).

Evidently, the prevailing sentiment is that if questions of a legal nature were to arise at a closing, an attorney would be the only party capable of answering these questions and that the public might be irreparably harmed if an attorney were not present to represent the buyer or borrower or a nonattorney attempted to provide answers.

Though a number of Signing Agents currently operate "under the radar" in attorney-only states, state bar and attorney associations vociferously and unequivocally oppose the practice of Notary Signing Agents conducting loan signings, and promise to prosecute offenders vigorously.

## Do I have to obtain a business license to operate as a Notary Signing Agent?

Due to the widely differing policies and laws of local municipalities, it is impossible to say with any certainty that a business license is or is not always required. The answer will depend upon the city in which you live or operate.

One of the complicating factors surrounding this question is that Notary Signing Agents can conduct business across city and county lines from transaction to transaction on a daily basis. Some Notaries even cross state lines to conduct a loan signing, if the Notary holds a commission in a state that issues appointments to nonresidents or resides in a state that has a reciprocity agreement with a neighboring state.

The best course of action is to investigate the matter by contacting the appropriate agency in your local municipality. You may discover, as is true of many cities, that the city charter contains a provision exempting Notaries Public from the requirement to carry a business license.

## Must I choose between obtaining assignments directly from lenders, escrow offices and title companies, or through a signing service; or can I do both?

As an independent contractor, a Notary Signing Agent is free to contract with assigning companies directly or utilize a signing service that brokers loan signing assignments. There is no need to choose just one or the other.

In fact, it is advantageous to work both ways. By obtaining your own assignments directly from assigning companies, you will be paid a higher fee than you will from a signing service. However, to obtain direct assignments, you must market your own services directly to these companies and that typically takes time, resources and a lot of hard work.

In addition to finding direct assignments, many Notary Signing Agents also cultivate a business relationship with a few select signing services with a reputation for compensating fairly and on time. Working with a signing service allows you to obtain signings without the same expenditure of time, effort and resources necessary for obtaining direct assignments. The trade-off is a lower fee per signing, but you should might of that as a marketing expense to obtain business.

The bottom line is that whether you obtain assignments directly from lenders, title companies and escrow offices at a higher fee or through signing services at a lower fee, you will incur marketing costs. You will either do the hard work to obtain business directly, or you will pay a signing service to bring you business.

## OBTAINING CLIENTS AND ASSIGNMENTS

### Can I affix my Notary stamp to a signing service application form?

Signing services and other companies enlisting Notary Signing Agents for home loan signing assignments commonly ask prospective Agents to provide proof of their notarial credentials. These firms request Notaries to fax, e-mail or mail a reproduction of the official seal as proof of commissioning.

On the surface it may appear harmless for a Notary to affix a seal impression on an application to provide services, and especially at a time when the Notary wants to comply with requests from a potential client. However, the sobering reality is that use of the official seal for any other purpose than performing official acts is an unwise practice if not an act prohibited by law. In California, the law expressly disallows any use of an official seal except to carry out the duties and responsibilities required of Notaries. In Oregon, the seal may not be used to promote any product, services or other offering. This means you can not use your official seal to promote your Notary Signing Agent Services.

As mortgage fraud is becoming more rampant, it is not difficult to imagine a photocopied image of the Notary's seal being lifted from a paper, manipulated with graphics software to make it appear as an actual seal impression, and used with intent to commit such fraud. Notaries in two states must be extra vigilant about this; in Nevada, Notaries are permitted to use as a seal a computerized seal image, and in Iowa, an adhesive label containing the information in the Notary's seal. However, all Notaries — and Notary Signing Agents in particular — should especially be alert to the risks of seal misuse. If a signing service or firm seeks confirmation of a Notary's commissioning, a photocopy of the official commission paper can be offered as proof or confirm proof of commissioning from the Secretary of State or other commissioning official instead.

## Can I negotiate provisions in an independent contractor's agreement? If there is a provision that I don't like, can I line through it or change it, and then sign?

As an independent contractor you are free to work for any company you want to contract with. You can also certainly ask if provisions in a contractor's agreement are open to discussion and negotiate them in your favor.

Chances are that if you line through or modify a clause, sign the agreement, and return the modified contract, the company may not choose to do business with you. The best course of action is to contact the owner or manager of the company by phone after you have had a chance to read through the agreement and ask if the company is amenable to modifying the specific provision causing concern. You may find that they are open to a reasonable compromise. If they are not willing to negotiate, you'll have to decide whether you are willing to work under the terms of the agreement or if the provision is a "deal-breaker" that precludes the possibility of a constructive business relationship.

**If I signed an independent contractor's agreement with a non-competition clause but then discover a client of mine is also a client of the signing service, will I have breached my contract?**

It will depend upon the precise language of the non-competition clause. You should consult an attorney who can provide guidance and counsel on specific matters.

"Non-compete" agreements are necessary to protect the investment the signing service has made to secure accounts with companies needing the services of Notary Signing Agents. It would be unfair and unethical for an Agent to enter into a non-compete agreement and then proceed to wrest business away from the signing service. Such a tactic can cause considerable damage that could form the basis of a lawsuit.

However, if you have already cultivated a prior business relationship with a client only to discover the client utilizes the signing service when they can't find a Notary Signing Agent directly, you should openly discuss your relationship with both companies. But the question deals with discoveries the client's relationship with the service _after_ signing. Perhaps you can arrive at a mutually satisfactory resolution to the problem: the signing service will honor your prior relationship with the client and you won't take signing assignments for the client through the signing service.

For more specific assistance, consult an attorney who can advise you of the legal ramifications of non-competition agreements in your state.

**Is compensation for my travel expenses included in the fee I am paid?**

Most companies pay a flat fee for a signing that includes all the services you perform — contacting the borrower, setting the appointment, traveling to and from the appointment, carrying out the signing, notarizing the documents, and couriering the documents for shipment to the closing agent.

**Do I need an office apart from my residence for my Notary Signing Agent business? Are there any benefits to having such an outside office?**

The nature of the Notary Signing Agent vocation is contact by phone. When you are not making or receiving phone calls, you'll be traveling to the office of a lender, title company or escrow agency to keep an appointment or make a contact. It is not likely that representatives from these companies will call on you at your office.

So, for many Notary Signing Agents an outside office is not required. However, there may be instances when an outside office is necessary to conduct business as a Signing Agent. For example, if you are seeking to perform loan signing assignments in a bordering state in which you do reside, you may be required to have a physical office or work address in the bordering state to obtain a nonresident Notary Public commission.

**Will Notary errors and omissions insurance cover me in the event the loan documents were not returned in a timely manner?**

Errors and omissions insurance only covers the Notary Signing Agent for the notarizations that he or she performs on applicable documents in a loan package. This insurance does not cover the Agent for failing to return documents or for other losses that result from the Agent's negligence in performing non-notarial Signing Agent duties.

**What are "e-mail docs"**

"E-mail docs" are documents in a loan package that are sent via electronic mail to a Notary Signing Agent, who then downloads and prints the documents for a signing assignment.

Transmitting e-mail docs saves costs in several ways. First, instead of having an escrow or title office print the documents and courier them to a Notary Signing Agent in advance of an appointment, the escrow or title company cuts out the delivery service, saving the costs of overnight shipping. Second, the escrow or title company is also spared the expense of duplicating the copies and preparing the packet.

Perhaps the biggest advantage of using e-mail to deliver loan documents is that it provides time-strapped lenders and closing offices more time to generate the loan package during high-volume peak periods. There is no longer the need to meet a shipping deadline of 5:00 p.m. the day before the signing.

While lenders and closing agents appreciate the extra time that they have to prepare packages, Notary Signing Agents often report that the extra time provides closing agents with an excuse to transmit the package at the very last minute, potentially wreaking havoc to Agents' time schedules. If you plan to accept e-mail docs, make sure you set a cut-off time when documents must be delivered, in order to ensure adequate time to print the documents and maintain control over your schedule.

A Notary Signing Agent who is set up to receive e-mail docs will receive a higher fee for the signing, since the Agent will prepare the package for the signing.

### What additional equipment do I need to have or purchase to accept e-mail docs?

First, you need a computer and a high-speed Internet connection to receive the loan package. The fast Internet connection is a must to reduce the time it takes to download the documents.

Second, you need a laser printer. An inkjet printer is generally not sufficient because it "sprays" ink on the page.

When choosing a laser printer, you should ensure that the printer meets the following minimum requirements:

1. The printer must be compatible with Hewlett Packard Printer Command Language (PCL) version 4+ or higher. Hewlett-Packard created the PCL printer command language to provide an economical and efficient way for

application programs to control a range of printer features across a number of printing devices. The PCL printer language is common to virtually all HP printers, and is incorporated into many non-HP laser printers as well.

2. The printer must have at least 5 megabytes (MB) of internal dedicated memory. Printer memory is important, since the documents must be queued into the printer's memory prior to printing.

3. The printer must be able to print letter and legal size documents. Ideally, the printer should have separate paper trays for each paper size and be able to automatically select the proper tray while the documents are printing.

Additional software programs must be installed on your computer, but these are typically provided by the lender or document preparer, and are free of charge. There are at least three methods by which e-mail docs are transmitted:

1. As Adobe® Reader files (PDF). Adobe® Reader can be downloaded from www.adobe.com.

2. By a third-party mortgage document packaging utility. eLynx (www.elynx.com) is one company providing software for the preparation of electronic documents. To print the file, you must download and install the printer utility software from eLynx's Web site.

3. Via Web site. With this option, Notary Signing Agents are directed to a secure Web site, enter the site by entering a user name and password and click on a link to download and print the documents. If you retrieve the documents from an online Web site, your computer may need to have a current version of Microsoft® Internet Explorer installed.

### Can I charge extra for accepting e-mailed documents? What is the going rate?

Most companies typically compensate Notary Signing Agents $25-$35 for accepting e-mailed documents. This fee is compensation for printing the documents and for incurring the cost of the printer and consumables (paper and toner).

Besides the hard costs associated with printing the documents, a key factor to weigh when setting a fee for e-mailed documents is the time it takes to print the job.

When setting your fee, keep in mind that many assignments may be last minute requests for loans that are date sensitive. Some Notary Signing Agents charge a premium for last minute requests.

Before setting a fee for accepting e-mail ad docs, make sure you understand any state laws that could affect what you may charge. In Nevada, Notary Signing Agents cannot charge an additional fee to print electronic documents.

Chapter

2

# Preparing for the Signing

## UNDERSTANDING INDUSTRY TERMS

**I have heard the terms "primary" and "secondary" mortgage markets used quite often. What exactly are these and how do they differ from one another?**

The "primary mortgage market" is the market where borrowers obtain loans from loan originators. The "secondary mortgage market" is the market where these mortgage loans are bought and sold.

Each market has its own "players" and "game". The players in the primary mortgage market include:

1. Mutual savings banks;

2. Commercial banks;

3. Savings and loan institutions;

4. Mortgage banks; and

5. Mortgage brokers.

With the exception of mortgage banks and brokers, the players in the primary mortgage market originate loans to sell in the secondary mortgage market or keep for their own investment. Mortgage banks and brokers originate loans to sell in the secondary market only.

The players in the secondary mortgage market include:

1. Government Sponsored Entities (GSE) "Fannie Mae," (Federal National Mortgage Association), "Freddie Mac" (Federal Home Loan Mortgage Corporation) and "Ginnie Mae" (Government National Mortgage Association).

2. Private investment banks; and

3. Investors, including pension funds, life insurance companies, commercial banks and thrifts.

There are three main options open to secondary mortgage market players:

1. A loan originator can both issue the loan and keep it for its own investment.

2. A loan originator can sell the loan directly to a secondary mortgage market investor.

3. A loan originator can sell loans to a GSE to bundle into mortgage backed securities, which the GSE then sells to investors.

Notary Signing Agents come into contact and interact with both primary and secondary mortgage market players. An Agent may receive an assignment for a loan signing from a bank, mortgage broker, or a signing service that has an account with a primary mortgage originator. The actual loan package that is signed by the borrower is issued by a loan originator. Thus, the Agent has a direct relationship with primary mortgage market players.

Notary Signing Agents interface with the secondary mortgage market as well, although the connection is indirect rather than direct. Since most loans are originated with a view toward selling them in the secondary market, Agents must ensure that all loan documents are signed correctly and that the notarizations are accurate and legible.

The presence of certain documents in a loan package can signal that the loan will be sold in the secondary market. Correction and compliance agreements are executed to ensure that all documentation conforms when secondary market investors consider purchasing the loan. Servicing agreements inform the borrower of the likelihood that the loan will be sold or serviced by another institution. Assignments of deeds of trust and mortgages appearing in a loan package indicate that the loan has been sold or transferred even before it is funded.

## What is the difference between a lender, a mortgage banker and mortgage broker?

A *lender* loans money to finance a home purchase, a refinance of an existing mortgage or a home equity line of credit. A lender can be a traditional brick and mortar bank, savings and loan association, mutual savings bank, credit union, thrift, life insurance company, financial services firm, professional or trade association, government agency, private financing company or even the seller.

A *mortgage banker* is a person or company whose principal business is the originating, financing, closing, selling and servicing of home loans for institutional lenders on a contractual basis. A mortgage banker is essentially synonymous with a lender.

A *mortgage broker* is a middleman or matchmaker, joining the home buyer or homeowner with a lender who can provide a loan. A mortgage broker charges a fee for recommending a loan program that best meets the needs of a client. The broker performs many of the same functions a lender would, including taking applications, ordering appraisals and title searches, verifying income and employment and checking credit.

Since a mortgage broker is not beholden to any one lender, a broker can shop around and find the best loan at the best rate.

Both mortgage bankers and brokers tout their unique advantages. Mortgage bankers assert that since the lender ultimately determines creditworthiness, why not go directly to the source and deal with the lender? Mortgage bankers emphasize that a direct lender can be more responsive to a borrower's needs and cut down valuable time in the loan process.

Mortgage brokers market their ability to draw from literally hundreds of lenders and loan programs to find the best loan for the home buyer or homeowner. Brokers emphasize that since they do not represent one company and one line of products, they can be more objective in advising clients.

## What is the Truth in Lending Act (TILA)?

The Truth in Lending Act is a federal statute that requires sellers and lenders to disclose credit terms and interest rates in an identical manner so borrowers can shop around to compare loans.

The Truth in Lending Act was enacted in 1968. Prior to TILA there were no generally required definitions of loan terms so that consumers were unable to compare interest rates and other loan costs. Scams and fraud were pervasive.

The Truth in Lending Act requires the disclosure of credit terms prior to entry into a consumer credit contract. These disclosures must be in writing. The Truth in Lending Act includes these important disclosures:

The Annual Percentage Rate (APR) — The APR is the interest rate that factors in all financial charges included in the loan. The APR is usually higher than the interest rate reflected in the "Note." Comparing the "APR" is the best way to comparison shop for loans.

The Amount Financed — The amount financed is the actual loan amount. It will often include various third party fees that are being financed, including fees for credit reports, appraisals, and warranties.

The Finance Charge — The finance charge is the total of all of the upfront finance charges, plus all the interest paid over the life of the loan. On a mortgage, the finance charge often exceeds the amount financed.

Total of Payments — The total of payments represents the total dollar cost of the loan, assuming the loan is repaid according to the schedule of payments.

Schedule of Payments — The schedule of payments itemizes the timing, number and dollar amount of payments due over the entire course of the loan.

## What is RESPA?

Enacted in 1974, the Real Estate Settlement Procedures Act (RESPA) is a federal consumer protection statute designed to help homebuyers be better shoppers in the home buying process. RESPA regulates settlement service providers, outlaws kickbacks that increase the cost of settlement services and requires that consumers receive disclosures at various times in the transaction. Some disclosures spell out the costs associated with the settlement, outline lender servicing and escrow account practices and describe business relationships between settlement service providers.

RESPA covers loans secured with a mortgage placed on a one-to-four family residential property. These include most purchase loans, assumptions, refinances, property improvement loans and equity lines of credit.

Disclosure forms required under RESPA that a Notary Signing Agent will handle during the course of executing a signing assignment include:

1. "Affiliated Business Arrangement Disclosure" (AfBA) — This disclosure is required whenever a settlement service provider involved in a RESPA-covered transaction refers the consumer to a provider with whom the referring party has an ownership or other beneficial interest. The AfBA disclosure describes the business arrangement that exists between the two providers and gives the borrower an estimate of the second provider's charges.

2. "Good Faith Estimate of Settlement Costs" (GFE) — The GFE represents to the borrower the estimated costs necessary to close the loan transaction. RESPA requires

that the GFE be supplied to the borrower within three business days of completion of the loan application, but oftentimes it will be included in the loan documentation package. "HUD-1 Settlement Statement" (HUD-1) — The HUD-1 is the de facto standard form that lists the actual settlement costs of the loan transaction.

3. "Initial Escrow Statement" — This disclosure itemizes the estimated taxes, insurance premiums, and other charges anticipated to be paid from the escrow account during the first twelve months of the loan.

4. "Servicing Transfer Statement" — This form is often included in the loan package if the lender has sold or assigned the servicing rights of the borrower's loan to another loan servicer. The notice must include the name and address of the new servicer, toll-free telephone numbers, and the date the new servicer will begin accepting payments.

## What is a "stipulation"?

In the loan signing context, a stipulation is a requirement the borrower must meet for the loan to be funded. Also known as a *condition*, common stipulations include pay stubs, W-2 or 1099 forms, hazard insurance declarations and checks for closing costs.

Notary Signing Agents are routinely asked to ensure that certain stipulations are met at the signing assignment. For example, the Agent may be requested to pick up a check for closing costs to include with the signed and notarized documents.

In certain cases, a lender or title company will even instruct Notary Signing Agents to halt the signing if the borrower does not produce a stipulation at the signing appointment. The most common stipulation of this kind is a verification of income (W-2, 1099 form, or pay stubs from past paychecks).

## What is a "lien" on the property?

A "lien" is a legal claim against property for monies owed, also known as a "security interest." A lien allows the creditors a means of preventing the property from being sold without the lien being paid.

The main types of liens are:

1. Mortgages and deeds of trust;

2. Tax liens (property, income, business, etc.);

3. Mechanics' liens (security to contractors who provided goods and services for building projects, renovation or remodeling projects); and

4. Judgment liens (court awards and judgments attaching to the property).

Most liens must be publicly recorded and the order in which they are recorded affects the priority of payment. For example, a mortgage is often considered the "first" lien on a property — the first claim that must be paid when the property is sold.

Notary Signing Agents may occasionally be asked to notarize a "Subordination Agreement," a document by which one creditor "subordinates" or postpones its claim to a second creditor until that creditor's lien has been satisfied.

## What is an "encumbrance"?

"Encumbrance" is a general term to signify any right, interest or other claim against real property that is registered on title and affects the owner's ability to sell the property.

Specific examples of encumbrances are mortgages, deeds of trust, recorded abstracts of judgment, unpaid real property taxes, tax liens, mechanic's liens, easements, water or timber rights and restriction on the use of the land.

## What does "P.O.C." stand for?

"P.O.C." is an acronym used in the mortgage industry to indicate the loan fees and charges that were "paid outside of closing."

You will see "P.O.C." on the "Uniform Settlement Statement," "Borrower's Estimated Settlement Statement" or "Good Faith Estimate of Settlement Charges" opposite a charge to mark that the cost has already been paid.

For example, fees for an appraisal, flood or termite inspection often must be paid at the time services are rendered and cannot be folded into the loan. All charges must be accounted for at closing, even P.O.C. charges. P.O.C. charges may be paid back to the applicant upon closing if the amounts are financed.

## What is the "Loan to Value Ratio?"

The "loan to value ratio" is the relationship expressed as a percentage between the "loan" amount and "value" of the property. The "L.T.V.," as it is commonly referred to, is an important benchmark in the mortgage loan industry.

In purchase transactions, a loan to value ratio of 80% or higher typically means a lender will require a borrower to carry private mortgage insurance until such time that the ratio drops below 80%. In refinance transactions, lenders will typically not refinance the property for higher than the industry standard loan to value ratio of 75%, which includes any cash out from the refinance.

## What is the "Housing Ratio?"

The "housing ratio" equals a combined monthly mortgage payment divided by gross monthly income. The monthly mortgage payment used in the calculation of the housing ratio includes the total of principal, interest, taxes and insurance (PITI) payments. Lenders use housing ratios to approve loan applicants.

For example, a combined monthly mortgage payment of $1,800 divided by gross monthly income of $6,000 equals a housing ratio of 30%; in this case, a borrower spends 30% of his gross monthly income on housing costs. Acceptable ratios vary by lender, but usually fall between 28% — the industry standard — and 40% at the highest end.

### What is an "assessed value"? Is it the same as the "appraised value"?

The "assessed value" is the value placed on property as a basis for establishing property taxes. The local tax assessor is the official tasked with valuing properties.

The taxing authority sets a tax rate — typically per each square foot of land — called the assessed tax rate. To calculate the assessed value, the size of the lot is multiplied by the tax rate.

The assessed value of property is not to be confused with the "appraised" value of property — an opinion of a property's fair market value based on an appraiser's knowledge, experience, analysis of the property and comparable sales of properties in the immediate area. The appraised value is used to set the purchase price of a home, to determine market value for determining refinance loans and to ascertain the appropriate amount of insurance to be purchased.

### What role does the appraiser play in a real property refinance or home equity line of credit transaction?

The role of the appraiser is to provide objective and unbiased opinions about the value of real property. The appraiser examines the property and submits a written report that generally consists of:

1. A description of the property and its surroundings;

2. An analysis of the "highest and best use" of the property;

3. An analysis of sales of comparable properties; and

4. Information regarding current real estate activity and/or market area trends.

The appraisal report assists those who own, manage, sell, invest in and/or lend money on the security of real estate.

Every state requires appraisers to licensed or certified in order to provide appraisals to federally regulated lenders.

### What is a "prepayment"?

A "prepayment" is an unscheduled payment of all or part of the outstanding principal of a mortgage loan before it is due.

Some mortgages have strict provisions penalizing borrowers for paying off the loan balance early. Such penalties can amount to as much as several percentage points. A common question that arises at a loan signing is whether the loan contains a prepayment penalty.

If a borrower wants to examine the prepayment provisions of the loan, the Notary Signing Agent should pull out the "Truth in Lending Disclosure" and promissory note, the two predominant documents with the prepayment provisions. In some instances, an addendum to the "Note" or rider to the deed of trust or mortgage will contain these provisions as well.

### What is the Annual Percentage Rate and why is it higher than the interest rate in the "Note"?

The Annual Percentage Rate (APR) is a rate, which is expressed as a yearly percentage rate and is a measure of the total cost of credit, including interest and other recurring charges.

The APR was established by the federal Truth in Lending Act (TILA) at a time when consumers found it difficult to comparison shop for the best loan. The APR was created to be a "shop around rate" that could be used in comparing the loans of competing lenders.

The APR is disclosed in the "Truth in Lending Disclosure Statement," a universal form that contains many of the federally required disclosures required by the TILA.

Notary Signing Agents should be aware that many borrowers confuse the APR with the interest rate of the loan and are startled when they are asked to sign the TILA disclosure at a loan signing. Agents should not attempt to explain precisely how the borrower's APR was calculated, but they can tell the borrower that the APR is generally higher than the interest rate for the loan. It often helps to pull out the "Note" at the same time the TILA disclosure is signed, so the borrower can confirm the actual interest rate for the loan.

Some lenders include an "APR Worksheet" with the loan documents so the borrower can examine how the APR was calculated. When this document is present in the loan package, the Agent should pull it out and present it to the borrower at the time the TILA disclosure is signed.

## How is the Annual Percentage Rate calculated?

The Annual Percentage Rate (APR) is calculated by spreading the costs of the private mortgage insurance (if applicable) and prepaid finance charges (loan discount, origination fees, prepaid interest, and other credit costs) over the life of the loan.

The APR differs from the interest rate because it includes one-time fees in an attempt to calculate a total cost of borrowing money. Thus, the APR is generally higher than the interest rate shown on the "Note."

Some consumer advocates maintain that the APR cannot calculate the true cost of borrowing money because many one-time fees incurred in the financing of real property are not factored into the APR. These fees include:

1. Appraisal fee;

2. Home-inspection fees;

3. Credit report costs;

4. Title fees;

5. Attorney and Notary fees; and

6. Document preparation fees.

## What are "points"?

In the broadest sense, a point is 1% of a loan amount. However, defined in narrower terms, "points" can be described in one or more of the following ways:

1. Origination points: A fee of 1% of the loan amount charged by the lender to cover the processing expenses for providing the loan. Origination points are paid by the borrower up front, either at closing or outside of closing.

2. Discount points: A fee paid at closing by the borrower to obtain a lower interest rate on the loan.

3. Negative points: A fee paid by a lender at closing to reduce the borrower's closing costs. Since high up-front costs are a barrier to homeownership for many buyers, negative points (also called "rebates") can effectively lower the barrier to entry into the market. When the lender pays points for the loan, the borrower opts for a higher interest rate to lower the settlement costs. To the extent such points are "reasonable," they are legal under the federal RESPA law. However, when a lender uses negative points as a means to artificially inflate interest rates or as a means of concealing referral payments to brokers, the practice — also called a "yield spread premium" — borders on the illegal.

## What is "P.I.T.I."?

P.I.T.I. stands for "Principal, Interest, Taxes, and Insurance," the four elements of a monthly mortgage payment. Payments of principal and interest are applied toward the loan balance while amounts for taxes and insurance satisfy local property taxes and the various insurance premiums as they become due.

Depending upon the type of loan, lender requirements, and/or homeowner preferences, the entire P.I.T.I. amount can be paid in one single monthly payment, with the amounts for taxes and insurance set aside into an impound or escrow account; or the borrower sets aside equivalent amounts for taxes and insurance and pays these bills directly on an annual or semi-annual basis.

## What is a "first" and "second" mortgage?

A first mortgage is the primary lien against a property. It has first priority over all other claims against the property except taxes and bond indebtedness. A second mortgage is one that has a lien position subordinate to the first mortgage.

## What is an "assumption option"?

An assumption option is a feature in a mortgage loan that allows a new applicant to take over an existing loan. The lender typically must approve the new buyer who agrees to assume liability.

Not all loans are assumable; in fact, most loans are not. With an assumable loan, the original borrower's liability may or may not be released. Unlike a traditional transaction where the new homeowner obtains a mortgage loan to pay off the existing "Note," an assumable loan does not need to be paid in full by the original borrower upon sale or transfer of the property.

Loans that have an assumption option contain an assumption *clause* within the promissory note and security instrument that states whether or not a potential buyer can assume responsibility for the mortgage from the existing borrower.

## What is an impound account?

An impound account is a trust type account established by the lender to set aside a portion of a homeowner's monthly mortgage payment to pay property taxes, private mortgage insurance premiums and hazard insurance policy premiums required to protect the home. Impounds are usually collected with the "Note" payment. Some loans require establishment of an impound account; in other cases the account may be optional.

## What does it mean when a transaction is "date sensitive?"

A transaction is considered "date sensitive" when documents must be signed on or by a particular date. Notary Signing Agents should treat every assignment as though it has to be completed on the day assigned and every attempt should be made to keep appointments as scheduled.

Signing services and title companies typically inform Notary Signing Agents when a transaction is date sensitive. The title agent or signing service representative may say, "This signing must be completed today," or "I have an assignment that must be signed either today or tomorrow." Some companies arrange a preset appointment with the borrower and tell the Agent that the appointment must be kept as scheduled.

There are three particular circumstances when the timing of the transaction must be forefront in the Agent's mind:

1. At the end of the month, especially on the last day of the month for signing loans with a rescission option. For a loan to close by month's end, three business days must transpire leading up to the last day of the month when the deed of trust or mortgage is recorded. It is critical that you know when this day falls, for the date will differ by month. Be especially mindful of this when scheduling "open" appointments and give yourself enough time to work under the deadline.

2. When a borrower must reschedule a preset appointment. This happens more often than you would think. When the borrower asks to reschedule, tell the borrower you will get back to him or her after you have called the assigning company to see if there is flexibility on the date of signing.

3. Weekend appointments. Keeping any rescission period in mind, rescheduling a Saturday appointment for Sunday to accommodate a borrower's plan may be acceptable since the rescission period will be the same no matter which of

the two days the signing appointment occurs. Nevertheless, you should check with the assigning company for their approval.

## What does the term "vesting" mean?

According to *Black's Law Dictionary* (7th Edition, 1999) the verb "vest" means "to confer ownership (of property) upon a person." "Vesting" refers to the manner or percentage of interest in which a person can hold this ownership of real property.

Depending upon the jurisdiction, there are several ways an ownership in real property can be vested, including:

1. <u>Tenancy in Common</u>: A method vesting title to property owned by any two individuals ("tenants") in undivided shares. Each tenant owns a share of the property, is entitled to a portion of the income from the property, and must bear a comparable share of expenses. Each co-tenant has the right to sell, lease or will the co-tenant's share of the property.

2. <u>Sole Ownership</u>: The vesting of title to an individual who is capable of acquiring title. For example, a single man may take title as "John Jason Schmidt, an unmarried man." Or, if married, he may take title as "John Jason Schmidt, a married man as his sole and separate property."

3. <u>Community Property</u>: The vesting of title only between a husband and wife as property acquired "in community" each other (*i.e.,* during the marriage). Separate interests cannot be conveyed. Conversely, "separate property" is property a spouse acquired prior to the marriage.

4. <u>Joint Tenancy</u>: Another form of co-ownership between two or more individuals. When a joint tenant dies, title to the property automatically passes to the surviving joint tenant(s) (called the "right of survivorship"). Therefore, a

joint tenant cannot will his or her interest in the property to an heir.

    5. <u>Community Property with Right of Survivorship</u>: An ownership interest between a husband and wife where title is automatically conveyed to the surviving spouse upon death of the other spouse.

Title to real property may also be vested in a corporation, partnership, or trust. Notary Signing Agents may encounter the latter when handling the signing of loan papers for a husband and wife who have created a family trust.

The vesting is found in the deed of trust or mortgage and in any conveyance deed (warranty, quitclaim, grant, bargain and sale) included in the loan document package.

The vesting is of importance to Notary Signing Agents in at least the following circumstances, which could determine the outcome of the signing appointment:

1. If the vesting contains typographical errors, the documents likely will have to be redrawn and signed at a future time. Agents should have borrowers carefully review and confirm the spelling of all names in the vesting. If there are errors, the title or escrow officer involved in the settlement should be contacted immediately.

2. If the method of acquiring title is different from what the borrowers expected or requested, the borrowers may elect to halt the signing until the vesting can be corrected. As with the former case, the title or escrow officer should be contacted before proceeding with the signing.

3. A borrower may have changed his or her legal name since the date he or she took title to the property. This is an issue in the case where a female borrower has married and acquired a driver's license or other primary identification document in the married name, but does not have an acceptable written identification card in the

former name. It is entirely possible an unmarried borrower may convey title to herself in the new married name, or to her husband and herself in the new married name.

## What is the difference between an "escrow state" and a "non-escrow state"?

The terms "escrow" and "non-escrow" states have been variously understood. According to one meaning, escrow states are states where it is legal for an escrow company to conduct the closing. Non-escrow states are states where an attorney must conduct the closing. Notary Signing Agents would be generally permitted to participate in closings in "escrow" states.

Another meaning defines "escrow state" as a state where there is not a "traditional" closing. The buyer and seller provide the escrow or title company with closing instructions and go into the escrow company separately to sign the necessary documents. The closing is then conducted by the escrow company, which informs both the buyer and the seller when closing occurs.

Funding of a loan and disbursement of the loan proceeds generally occur much quicker in escrow closing states, where the loan is normally funded after the signed documents have been received back by the lender.

In "non-escrow" states, the buyer and seller closings take place simultaneously with both parties normally present at the same table. Funds are brought to the closing by the buyer and disbursed to the seller at the closing.

## What does it actually mean when a document is "recorded"?

Document recording is the process of placing a document in the local county, city or township public records office overseen by a public official known as the county recorder, recorder of deeds, register of deeds or auditor.

Some of the common documents that are placed in the public records include:

1. Deeds to real property;

2. Mortgages and deeds of trust;

3. Mortgage releases, assumptions, encumbrances, assignments, subordinations and waivers of priority

4. Certificates of transfer, including affidavits, easements and leases;

5. Certificate of title to registered land;

6. Land contracts;

7. Plats (drawings showing location of lots and boundaries of subdivided land);

8. Partnerships, powers of attorney and trusts;

9. Zoning resolutions, maps and amendments;

10. Annexations, petitions, state centerline surveys and street name changes

11. Military service discharges;

12. Financing statements (filed under provisions in the Uniform Commercial Code);

13. Corporation mergers, name changes, cancellations and bills of sale;

14. Liens: Mechanic's liens and notices of commencement, unemployment compensation liens, workers' compensation liens and tax liens.

It is commonly supposed that recording a deed is required by law in order for ownership to transfer from the seller to the buyer. In fact, transfer occurs once a deed has been signed, sealed and delivered to the purchaser. Recording the deed is necessary to protect the purchaser from future claims on the title and helps resolve disputes between multiple grantees or buyers.

Document recording imparts *constructive notice* of ownership. Constructive notice is notice that is given to the public by recorded documents. Possession of property is also considered constructive notice that the person in possession has an interest in the property.

Once recorded, a deed becomes part of the property's chain of title. Any member of the public can look up the property and find who the official owner is. As a potential purchaser of real property, how do you know that seller truly owns title to property? How do you determine that the seller hasn't previously conveyed the property to someone else? You would conduct a title search by examining the recording system maintained by your county's central registry of deeds.

## UNDERSTANDING LOANS

### What is a fixed mortgage rate?

A fixed mortgage rate is an interest rate that does not change for a specified term.

A "fixed rate mortgage" usually refers to a fully amortized mortgage with a fixed interest rate for the life of the loan (typically 30 years). However, fixed rate mortgages are available for 20-, 15- and even 10-year terms. The lower the term length for the loan, the lower the fixed rate is.

In addition to fixed rate mortgages, there are many different adjustable rate loan products available that carry a fixed interest rate for a portion of the loan term (1, 3, 5, 7 years). After the initial fixed rate period, the loan converts to an adjustable rate mortgage (ARM) for the remaining term of the loan.

During the refinance boom of the early 2000s, the lowest interest rates in decades drove large numbers of homeowners to refinance their existing ARM or higher fixed rate mortgages into lower fixed rate loans. Many homeowners who had 30-year fixed rate mortgages obtained low fixed rate loans with 20- and 15-year terms. The lower interest rates enabled these borrowers to retain essentially the same monthly mortgage payment as before, while cutting the length of the loan term by one third or even one half.

As the refinance boom subsided, lenders began to more aggressively market ARM mortgages and home equity lines of credit.

## What is an Adjustable Rate Mortgage (ARM) loan?

Also known as a *variable rate mortgage*, an adjustable rate mortgage is a loan in which the interest rate is tied to a specific index that fluctuates periodically. The index tracks the approximate change in the cost of money over time. Because the interest rate is tied to a changing index, the interest rate — and therefore the payments — will change often over the term of the loan.

Most ARMs start out with an initial short-term fixed rate that is typically lower than the prevailing interest rate on a traditional 30-year fixed rate mortgage. Initial fixed rate periods include 1-, 3-, 5-, 7- and 10-year options. After the initial fixed rate period ends, the interest rate will adjust every year as the index changes.

When you see adjustable rate mortgages advertised as "1/1," "3/1," "5/1," "7/1" and "10/1" loans, it means the fixed initial rate is for 1, 3, 5, 7 and 10 years respectively, and after the fixed rate period ends, the loan rate adjusts yearly.

## What is a HELOC loan?

HELOC stands for home equity line of credit. It is a loan set up as an open or revolving line of credit, rather than for a fixed dollar amount. Most HELOC loans are second mortgages secured by a second deed of trust or mortgage on the property. In many loan signing assignments, Notary Signing Agents are asked to handle both a primary refinance and a HELOC loan (called a "double signing").

Many HELOC loans require the borrower to take an initial draw — say, $25,000 — which can be used for any conceivable purpose. Many HELOCs have a stated draw period, during which the borrower can use the line, and a repayment period during which it must be repaid. Repayment periods are usually 10 to 20 years, but some HELOCs require that the entire balance be repaid at the end of the draw period or contain a single balloon payment.

## What are the differences between FHA, VA and conventional loans?

FHA and VA loans are guaranteed by the government. FHA loans are backed by the Federal Housing Administration, while VA loans are backed by the Veterans Affairs Administration.

FHA loans are popular among first-time home buyers and families with limited resources for a down payment. An FHA loan only requires a 3 percent down payment. FHA loans are available for purchasing a new home or for financing an investment property. However, FHA loans typically require the borrower to obtain private mortgage insurance until the level of equity in the property reaches 20 percent.

VA loans are administered by the U.S. Department of Veterans Affairs. As the name implies, to qualify for a VA loan you must be a veteran, reservist, on active duty or a surviving spouse of a veteran with 100 per cent entitlement. Qualified buyers can use a VA loan to purchase a home with no money down, no cash reserves, no application fee, and reduced closing costs. In some instances a VA loan can be obtained for refinancing a current mortgage.

Unlike FHA and VA loans, a "conventional" loan is not insured by the federal government. To qualify for a conventional loan, a 20 percent down payment is typically required.

## What is a "balloon" mortgage?

A balloon mortgage is a loan that is repaid in a series of small, periodic payments for a short period of time (e.g., 7 years), after which the entire balance comes due in a single, large "balloon" sum. If the borrower defaults on the balloon payment, the home is foreclosed.

Borrowers opt for balloon mortgages in situations where they know they will not reside in the home for more than the shortened loan term or plan to refinance later to obtain a more favorable traditional loan.

A balloon mortgage is not the same as an adjustable rate mortgage (ARM). ARM loans are traditionally amortized mortgages (30, 25, 15-years) where the interest rate adjusts periodically, resulting in higher (or lower) monthly payments. Unlike a balloon mortgage, the principal is not due at a predetermined date in one lump sum.

## What is a "reverse mortgage"?

A "reverse" mortgage or, more technically, a Home Equity Conversion Mortgage (HECM), is an unique loan product — so named because it "reverses" the typical borrower-to-lender loan payment stream — allowing qualified seniors age 62 and older to convert the equity in their homes into a regular monthly source of income or a line of credit. In a reverse mortgage, seniors do not make regular monthly principal and interest payments to the lender; rather, the lender makes payments to the qualifying seniors who own their homes outright or have sufficient equity to tap.

Reverse mortgages differ from conventional loans in other ways as well. Unlike a conventional loan, repayment is postponed as long as the borrower lives in the home. The lender recoups its investment, plus accumulated interest and fees, from the proceeds of the sale at the time the home is sold. Any remaining equity proceeds in the home after repayment belongs to the homeowner or the homeowner's heirs.

In another benefit to seniors with fixed incomes, default, eviction or foreclosure is never a worry, since there are no monthly payments to miss.

**If a borrower elects to establish an impound or escrow account, does the borrower always pay the same amount into the account each month?**

Yes; the borrower will pay the exact amount indicated for the period specified in the "Initial Escrow Account Disclosure." This form provides the borrower with a running total of the activity in the impound account over the future twelve month period.

Sometimes borrowers ask if the amount paid into an impound account will change. After the first year the amount may change depending upon the individual's situation. For example, if a borrower adds a room to the house, the local tax authority may reassess the property and levy additional property taxes. Conversely, once a borrower has built up sufficient equity in the property, an impounded amount for private mortgage insurance may be erased, resulting in lower impounds each month.

The operative term of the "Initial Escrow Account Disclosure" is the word "initial." The form covers the 12-month period beginning with the month of the first payment on the loan.

## UNDERSTANDING LOAN DOCUMENTS

**I am a Notary in a state where it is illegal to notarize an incomplete document. If the legal description paragraph in a deed of trust or mortgage says, "See Exhibit A attached hereto and made a part hereof," must I make sure the "Exhibit A" is present and complete?**

Yes; the "Exhibit A" must be present for the deed of trust or mortgage (security instrument) to be considered complete. Without it, the borrower in essence is being asked to sign — and the Notary Signing Agent to notarize — a document with a gaping blank space.

Unfortunately, it is the practice of many closing agents to ship the loan documents to the Notary Signing Agent without the referenced exhibit, expecting Agents to notarize the security instrument, and return the signed documents back. At the last minute before taking the deed of trust or mortgage to the county recorder or register of deeds' office, the closing agent then slips the exhibit in at the proper place.

In cases where the exhibit is not present, Notary Signing Agents can:

1. Call the closing agent and ask to have the legal description faxed over before the appointment. Most closing agents will do this — some begrudgingly — to accommodate the needs of the Notary Signing Agent.

2. Look to see if there is a "Preliminary Title Report" in the package of loan documents. Quite often there is a legal description of the property included in this report. You can then call the closing agent and ask if it would be acceptable to photocopy the legal description to include with the deed of trust or mortgage as the missing exhibit.

3. Search for a "cover sheet" to the deed of trust or mortgage. This cover sheet contains a summary of all necessary information for the security instrument to be properly indexed and recorded in the local land records. If the cover sheet contains the legal description, then you are in business. You can always contact the closing agent to confirm the correct description.

The goal with any of these strategies is to obtain the missing legal description prior to the appointment so that the security instrument will not contain a blank where the description should appear. Without a proper legal description present, the borrower will not know for certain if the security instrument the borrower is signing refers to the correct property. The borrower has every right to verify the correct property is being pledged as security for the loan.

As a Notary, you have every right to demand that the description be there and to refuse to notarize the security instrument until the exhibit is provided. Closing agents across the country will not modify their practice unless principled

Notary Signing Agents insist the legal description be included in the package.

## Am I responsible for the completeness of documents that aren't notarized?

One or more documents may require completion at the signing appointment, including, but not limited to, the following:

1. "Closing Instructions," a form in which the borrower is asked to provide the name and contact information for the insurance company providing hazard insurance on the property. The Instructions may also contain a section where the borrower is asked to indicate how he or she wants to receive excess closing funds after the settlement.

2. "Notice of Right to Cancel," where the correct rescission period commencement and termination dates must be provided.

3. "Statement of Information" form, asking the borrower for personal information on residences, marriages, and employment during the past ten years.

4. "Impound Account Authorization," a form in which the borrower is asked to check whether or not to establish an impound account for the payment of property taxes and insurance.

5. U.S. PATRIOT Act "CIP" form required of all financial institutions opening accounts with new customers. The Notary Signing Agent must record the personal identifying information taken from the borrower's state-approved photographic identification card in this form.

6. "IRS Form W-9," where in certain instances the form does not list the borrower's Social Security number and the borrower must insert the number into the form.

7. "Preliminary Change of Ownership Report," a document accompanying a conveyance deed that contains several questions related to the transfer of the property county recorders need to facilitate the recording of the deed.

In most cases, Notary Signing Agents should ensure the completeness of these forms, but this does not mean Agents are required to complete the forms themselves. The best course of action is to always have a contact number for the loan or closing agent available at the signing appointment to call if the borrowers needs guidance in completing a form.

## What is a "rider" to the deed of trust or mortgage?

The majority of deeds of trust and mortgages contain "uniform" or "boilerplate" language that changes little from transaction to transaction. Often there is need to amend the security instrument with specific provisions not covered in the uniform instrument. These additions (or deletions) are contained in one or more "riders" to the deed of trust or mortgage.

Examples of riders include:

1. Condominium Rider;

2. Adjustable Rate Rider;

3. 1-4 Family Rider;

4. Balloon Rider;

5. Prepayment Rider;

6. Construction Loan Rider;

7. Biweekly Payment Rider; and

8. Second Home Rider.

## What is the similarity and difference between a mortgage and deed of trust?

The main similarity between a mortgage and deed of trust is that both are *security instruments* — they pledge the property as security for the loan and are linked to the promissory note, the actual instrument of indebtedness.

It is the process of foreclosure which constitutes the most significant difference between a mortgage and a deed of trust.

In a mortgage, the borrower promises to repay the loan by pledging the property as collateral. A lien is placed on the title in favor of the lender until the debt is repaid. If the borrower defaults on the loan, the lender must initiate a legal foreclosure in the courts to recoup its investment, a process called "judicial" foreclosure. A mortgage is a two-party contract.

The so-called "mortgage states" include: Alabama, Arkansas, Connecticut, Delaware, Florida, Guam, Hawaii, Illinois, Indiana, Iowa, Kansas, Kentucky, Louisiana, Maine, Massachusetts, Michigan, Minnesota, New Hampshire, New Jersey, New Mexico, New York, North Dakota, Ohio, Oklahoma, Puerto Rico, Pennsylvania, Rhode Island, South Carolina, South Dakota, Vermont, Virgin Islands, Wisconsin and Wyoming.

In a deed of trust, the borrower grants and conveys the property to a third party (the "trustee"). The trustee holds title to the property until the loan obligation is fully satisfied. If the borrower defaults on the loan, the lender (the "beneficiary") informs the trustee of the default, who can invoke the power of sale on the property, a process called "nonjudicial" foreclosure. Unlike a mortgage, a judicial foreclosure is not necessary, since the borrower grants to the trustee the ability to sell the property to recover the lender's losses.

The so-called "deed of trust states" include: Alaska, Arizona, California, Colorado, District of Columbia, Idaho, Maryland, Mississippi, Missouri, Montana, Nebraska, Nevada, North Carolina, Oregon, Tennessee, Utah, Virginia, Washington, and West Virginia.

While most states fall into one of these two categories, there are a few states that accept either a mortgage or deed of trust as the security instrument.

The security instrument in the state of Georgia is called a "Security Deed." The "Security Deed" gives the Lender a security interest in property or real estate, providing the Lender the opportunity to seize the property in the event of default by the Borrower. The "Security Deed" is sometimes called a "Deed to Secure Debt," "Trust Deed" or "Land Contract." Foreclosures in Georgia are non-judicial.

## Does the borrower sign an "Assignment of Deed of Trust (Mortgage)" appearing in the loan package, and am I supposed to notarize the borrower's signature?

The borrower does not sign the "Assignment of Deed of Trust (Mortgage)" and the Notary Signing Agent does not notarize the form.

Lenders or holders of mortgages and deeds of trust often "assign" these instruments to other lenders or third parties. The "assignee" (designated person or company receiving the assignment) takes the place of the original lender or "assignor." To assign a deed of trust or mortgage, a written assignment must be drawn in proper form and recorded to provide public notice of the fact.

The assignment instrument is often included in the loan document package to facilitate the transfer once the loan has closed. It is meant to be signed and notarized at a later date.

In situations where an "Assignment of Deed of Trust (Mortgage)" is present, there may also be a "Notice of Assignment, Sale or Transfer of Servicing Rights" form as well. This document notifies the borrower of the assignment, sale, or transfer to the future named third party. This form must be signed by the borrower.

## I have noticed that there are loans I am asked to handle that do not contain a "Notice of Right to Cancel" form. Why is this? Are there transactions in which the right to cancel the transaction does not apply?

The primary scenarios where a rescission right applies are those most often encountered by Notary Signing Agents: refinance loans where the borrower is changing lenders, home equity loans or lines of credit, and "cash-out" refinance loans (loans for more than the current loan balance, and taking the difference in cash) with a different lender.

The following are circumstances when a mortgage loan does not have a rescission option:

1. When the loan is used to buy a house (known as a "purchase" transaction).

2. For refinance loans with the same lender.

3. When the home is not a primary residence (e.g., vacation home or investment property).

4. When the money borrowed is used for a private business.

5. When the lender is a state agency.

6. For "piggyback loans" — taking out a first and second mortgage loan — intended to avoid incurring private mortgage insurance.

7. For "cash-out" refinance loans with the same lender, only the cash-out portion can be rescinded.

**If the lender is required to send the "Good Faith Estimate" to the signer no more than 3 business days after applying for the loan, will the signer have already received a copy of this document before the signing?**

Maybe. The federal Real Estate Settlement Procedures Act (RESPA) did not envision the lending frenzy of the early 2000s where a borrower could apply for a loan and sign closing documents within a week or two. RESPA also could not anticipate the heavy volume of transactions the mortgage lending industry handled during the same time.

The result of the accelerated lending environment has meant that often a borrower may see the "Good Faith Estimate" and "Truth in Lending Disclosure" for the very first time at the actual signing appointment.

### What is the "Truth in Lending Statement"?

The "Truth in Lending Statement" is the written disclosure required under the federal Truth in Lending Act. It includes the Annual Percentage Rate (APR), the amount financed, the finance charge, the total of all payments and the schedule of payments in one easy to read form. This document is required in every mortgage loan and will appear in virtually every loan package. Along with the "Note," the "Truth in Lending Statement" contains a summary of all important terms of the loan. Notary Signing Agents often refer borrowers to this form to confirm the prepayment provisions and to answer other questions that arise at a loan signing appointment.

### I've noticed that some loan packages contain a "Borrower's Estimated Settlement Statement" while others contain the "HUD 1" Settlement Statement. Are these two documents one and the same?

The "HUD-1" and the "Borrower's Settlement Statement" are two forms of settlement statements. The federal Real Estate Settlement Procedures Act (RESPA) requires the U.S. Department of Housing and Urban Development Uniform Settlement Statement (HUD-1) to be used as the standard real estate settlement form in all 1-4 family residential transactions which involve federally-related mortgage loans between a borrower and a seller. The HUD-1 must be used in every RESPA-covered transaction, unless its use is specifically exempted. The HUD-1 is not required for home equity loans covered under the Truth in Lending Act. However, the HUD-1 is viewed as the industry standard and is often used in refinance transactions and in privately funded loans as well.

The HUD-1 and "Borrower's Estimated Settlement Statement" are not identical, but they serve the same purpose. They both list the borrower's closing costs.

## Why do some loan signing packages contain 2 or more "Good Faith Estimates," "Truth in Lending Disclosures," and "1003 Universal Loan Applications"?

If you look at each form closely, you'll probably see that each disclosure carries a different date. If so, then it is likely that the borrower has been negotiating with the lender over a number of months and is only now ready to consummate the loan transaction.

According to federal law, every time an interest rate change will affect the borrower's application, or every time the borrower changes a loan program, new versions of the federally-required disclosures must be generated. For example, you might notice that, in addition to differing dates on the various disclosures, the "Truth in Lending Statements" might contain a higher (or lower) APR, loan amount, finance charge, etc. The amount of closing costs could vary as well, so that is why the additional "Good Faith Estimates" are included.

All of the disclosures must be retained in the borrower's file, so if these forms have not been previously signed prior to the signing appointment, they are added to the closing documents to be executed at that time.

## What is the "Fair Lending Notice"?

State and federal laws prohibit financial institutions from discriminating in their lending services. The loan package will contain one or more disclosure forms for the borrower to sign, including the "Fair Lending Notice."

Under the provisions of the federal Fair Housing Act, it is unlawful to engage in the following practices based on race, color, national origin, religion, sex, familial status or handicap:

1. Refuse to make a mortgage loan;

2. Refuse to provide information regarding loans;

3. Impose different terms or conditions on a loan, such as different interest rates, points, or fees;

4. Discriminate in appraising property; and

5. Refuse to purchase a loan or set different terms or conditions for purchasing a loan.

## I conducted a loan signing in which the borrower signed two grant deeds. The borrower signed one as trustee of the family trust granting the property to himself individually, and the other as an individual granting the property to himself as trustee of the family trust. Why the need for two grant deeds?

Family trusts are created for the disposition of valuable assets with minimal tax consequences. A trust is created by executing a legal document that allows you to transfer ownership of your titled property from your individual name to a trust which you control. As a result, when you die your family avoids the delays and expenses of probate, the assets can be distributed quickly and all "business" is private and confidential.

Two grant deeds were needed because, while the property was vested in the trust, the debt of the loan is incurred by the individuals themselves. To pay off the old loan and acquire the new loan, title must be conveyed to the parties individually. Once the new loan is assumed, the individuals can convey title back to the family trust.

## What is a "Customer Identification Program" (CIP) form?

Effective October, 2003, the U.S. PATRIOT Act requires all qualifying financial institutions to obtain personal identifying information on all new account holders. Lenders, banks, title companies and escrow offices involved in mortgage loans qualify as a financial institution and must comply with U.S. PATRIOT Act regulations.

The personal identifying information is obtained for the purpose of checking a watch list of known or suspected terrorists engaged in money laundering or other illicit financial dealings to fund terrorism against the United States.

If the bank or lender has not obtained a new borrower's personal identifying information, Notary Signing Agents are requested to acquire this information at the loan signing appointment by completing a special PATRIOT Act "CIP" with the information taken from the borrower's driver license or passport.

## What is a "Hardship Letter"?

The "Hardship Letter" is a letter signed by the borrower and given to the lender stating that the debt of the loan will not cause undo hardship to the borrower. In particular, most hardship letters submitted in connection with loans that require the first mortgage payment to be paid within 30 days of the settlement specifically state that incurring the first payment within 30 days of the closing will not be a hardship to the borrower.

## ASSIGNMENT LOGISTICS

## What is a "double signing?"

"Double signing" is the term used to refer to a loan assignment involving two loans — a first and a second mortgage, for example. A double signing is also referred to as a "piggy-back" signing.

When asked to handle a double signing, there will be separate sets of documents for each loan. Depending upon the lender or lenders, the papers in each set could vary dramatically. Most second mortgages and home equity lines of credit (HELOC) loans contain less paperwork than the typical refinance loan.

Double signings take longer than transactions where one loan is involved, since there are two sets of papers, more notarizations, journal entries, etc.

When performing a signing with two loans, the NNA recommends that you complete the journal entries for both loans before the borrower signs the papers. And, it makes most sense to execute the first set of papers before the second mortgage or HELOC papers are signed.

Fees for double signings vary. Many signing services will pay a full fee for the first set of papers and one-half of the full fee for the second set. The rationale for paying one-half for the second loan is that the Notary Signing Agent incurs travel and couriering expenses once, not twice. However, many Agents request a full fee to execute both sets of papers.

### Should I have the borrower sign the borrower's copies as well as the originals?

Generally, no; only the originals must be signed. The borrower's copies are given unsigned to the borrower.

However, the National Notary Association recommends that the borrower's copies of the "Notice of Right to Cancel" be completed with the actual rescission period dates and executed in the same manner as the originals.

### What's the best place to conduct a signing? Can a Notary Signing Agent dictate where the signing should take place?

The most ideal spot to conduct a signing is in a borrower's home at a dining room table. A kitchen table is also fine, except there are often more distractions in the kitchen than in a dining room. The truth be told, Notary Signing Agents have conducted signings in living rooms, dens, outside on a patio, in the garage — just about every conceivable place in the house — except bathrooms!

An Agent should accommodate the borrower — within reason. Under no circumstances is a bedroom an appropriate place to stage a signing, unless it is necessary to service a bedridden signer.

That said, Agents will often arrive in homes where workers are present, nails are being hammered and carpet is being laid. You should be prepared to conduct the signing at any available horizontal space. Borrowers are often apologetic when renovations cause inconveniences and make it impossible to be dirt and distraction free, but Agents can put a borrower at ease by demonstrating understanding and a willingness to be flexible.

While most Agents will travel to a borrower's home or office to conduct the signing appointment, female Agents may request that the signing take place in a public place if it is prudent to do so.

## Does it matter if I use blue or black pens?

Some lenders require documents to be signed with blue ball point pens to more clearly distinguish the original loan documents from photocopies. Interestingly, there are other lenders who are equally adamant about signing documents with black pens.

Notary Signing Agents should carry an ample supply of pens of both colors. Usually special instructions for the signing will note whether a specific color of pen is required.

In the absence of a particular instruction, Notary Signing Agents can choose the color of pen to use or ask borrowers which color they prefer. In these cases, it is advisable that all parties, including the Notary Signing Agent, use the same color pen.

## What are some practical tips for saving time during a loan signing?

Since Notary Signing Agents are paid per signing, saving time during a loan signing is an important concern. There are some proven techniques for reducing the time spent at a signing which will enable you to take on more assignments, become more efficient, and be more profitable.

1. Ask the borrower to complete the "Statement of Information" before you arrive. If the borrower has access to a fax machine, offer to fax over the "Statement of Information" and any additional forms that require time and effort to complete.

2. Inform the borrower how long the signing should take. When you set the appointment, inform the borrower that you'll need "30 to 45 minutes max" for signing of the papers. Once at the table, reiterate that this should take "30 to 45 minutes at the most."

3. Sign the "Hot Button" documents first. "Hot Button" documents are those documents a borrower will scrutinize more closely and take longer to sign. Experience proves that the settlement statement, "Notice of Right to Cancel" form, "Note," and security instrument can raise the most questions. Executing these documents first can get the signing off on a fast track and prevent the signing from bogging down later. If the "Notice of Right to Cancel" form is signed early on, you can always refer back to the rescission period when a borrower stops to read a document.

4. At the midway point, offer to take a quick break. Some signings involve more documents than others and taking a quick "stretch break" can actually help speed up the signing. There are several reasons you may want to do this. First, when attention and concentration wanes, the tendency is to slow down. A quick break can help a borrower refocus on the task at hand. Second, you can use that time to check over the documents that have already been signed and, if the package contains many notarizations, catch up on reviewing these as well. Third, by offering to take a break, a borrower may respond, "No, I'm doing fine. Let's plow forward and get this done."

5. Take your cue from the borrower and adjust accordingly. Some borrowers are methodical by nature; this is

especially true of elderly signers. While in general it is not a good idea to rush a signer, you can assist an elderly signer who cannot quickly turn pages by offering to turn them. You'll discover many borrowers won't want to take long to sign the documents. The challenge in these cases is not to rush signing to the point where you are more susceptible to making mistakes.

At the conclusion of a signing appointment, always take an extra minute to personally thank the borrower for their help and assistance, no matter if you are in a hurry or not. And always ask, "Is there any other way I can assist you before I leave?"

### How long should a typical loan signing take?

New Notary Signing Agents should plan to spend an hour per appointment; experienced Agents 30 to 45 minutes. These timeframes are estimates and can vary from assignment to assignment based upon one or more of the following factors:

1. Obviously, some loans involve more paperwork than others, especially those loans that will be quickly sold in the secondary market. On the other hand, some home equity line of credit loans contain few papers and can be completed rather quickly — in under 20 minutes.

2. Double signings involve two sets of papers, which will take a little longer to complete.

3. If a person is signing as attorney in fact for an absent borrower, it will take longer to execute the signing because the attorney in fact will have to sign every signature as "William John Benson by Rosemary June Benson, his attorney in fact."

4. Distractions at the appointment, such as phone calls and the needs of small children, can cause a signing to take longer.

5. Packages with many notarizations will also take longer, since there will be more journal entries to record and notarial certificates to complete.

6. Some Notary Signing Agents work at a faster clip than others.

Individual signing assignments may take longer than others. Instead of expecting every signing to take the same amount of time, Notary Signing Agents should strive to adopt practices that will result in shorter signing appointments over time.

A helpful analogy is to think of the time spent at a signing appointment like a baseball player's batting average. A .300 batting average doesn't necessarily mean a player gets a hit 3 out of every 10 times at the plate. There may be games during a season where the batter hits .500 (2 hits in 4 plate appearances) and others where the batter hits. 250 (1 hit in 4 plate appearances). The goal over the course of a season is to maintain or exceed the .300 average taking into account both hitting "streaks" and "slumps."

Applied to Notary Signing Agents, some appointments may take longer, others shorter. The goal is to achieve a better "average" over the course of a period of time. Adopting a "big picture" view of time spent at signings will free you from the tyranny of the urgent and rushing signings that should be allowed to proceed at their own natural pace.

### Is it acceptable to conduct a signing at a local restaurant, coffee shop or other public place?

Absolutely. A borrower may request to meet at a restaurant because of construction at the family home or the presence of distractions which would make it difficult to concentrate on the signing of documents. Female borrowers, in particular, may wish to schedule the signing in a public place. Notary Signing Agents should accommodate the signer in these circumstances.

**If a complete set of borrower's copies are not included in the loan document package, am I required to make a copy for the borrower?**

Providing a borrower with a full set of copies is the responsibility of the lender or closing company. It is the practice of most lenders to include a full set of copies that the Notary Signing Agent can leave with the borrower.

The borrower's set of copies is often distinguished from the originals by various means, including:

1. Placement in a separate legal-size document folder;

2. Presence of a stamp marking the set as "Borrower's Copy"; and

3. Printing all of the borrower's copies on legal-size paper. (The originals often are printed on both letter- and legal-size paper, depending upon lender, title company, or county recorder requirements.)

Absence of a set of borrower's copies can result in the signing appointment taking longer than it otherwise would. Without a set of copies to review after the appointment, a borrower may feel more inclined to study the documents before signing them. For this reason, if a set of copies is not included in the package you should contact the assigning company to inquire whether you should provide a duplicate set and confirm that you will be reimbursed for the expense.

At the very least, you must always provide the borrower with 2 copies of the "Notice of Right to Cancel," since federal law requires that the borrower be provided 2 copies of this form when it is signed.

Some Notary Signing Agents have observed that lenders and closing companies do not include copies of certain documents. Examples include conveyance deeds executed with the loan documents and some title company forms. Often the lender will not include a copy of the borrower's loan application.

Conveyance deeds are returned to the original grantor, which may account for the reason why lenders will not include a copy of this document. As for the others, if a borrower notes that a copy of a particular form is not included, the Notary Signing Agent can offer to make a copy for the borrower after the signing or direct the borrower to the lender, who can provide the copy.

**When it says at the bottom of the Settlement Statement that the borrower needs to bring funds in at closing, is it absolutely necessary that I pick up a check?**

This question does not admit an easy answer. Several points must be made.

First, obviously, the funds must be received by the office conducting the settlement before the transaction can close.

Second, in the majority of residential transactions involving Notary Signing Agents — refinance loans and home equity lines of credit — there is a three-day right of rescission period that must elapse before the security instrument (Deed of Trust or Mortgage) can be recorded and the loan is funded. If the borrower does not bring a check to the signing appointment, usually the borrower can mail or deliver the check to the office responsible for the settlement prior to the end of the rescission period with little or no consequences.

When there is a rescission option for a loan, there is breathing room to compensate for cases when you are unable to pick up a check. Typical cases might include a borrower not wishing to pay settlement funds until a dispute over costs is reconciled, a miscommunication about costs or the borrower's inability to make it to the bank to obtain a cashier's check before the signing appointment, etc.

Third, if the transaction is a purchase transaction, a transaction involving investment property or a refinance of a second home, there is no rescission period. In these cases, a failure to pick up a check could cause a delay in the closing that could adversely affect the transaction.

Imagine the following fairly typical date-sensitive transaction: A loan must be closed the day following the signing appointment to avoid expiration of an interest rate lock. The Notary Signing Agent carries through with the signing appointment as scheduled, drops the documents off at a FedEx station by 5:00 p.m. to be delivered overnight to the settlement agent the next morning. The settlement agent anticipates recording the security instrument by early afternoon and closing the loan by the end of the business day.

In this situation, failure to collect the check for closing costs could prevent the loan from closing according to schedule, jeopardizing the rate lock.

Finally, a word should be mentioned about the so-called "licensure" states. Only a properly licensed Notary Signing Agent may conduct business in a state that allows only licensed settlement service providers to handle funds. In Virginia, for example, any Notary who picks up a check at a loan signing to return with the signed documents must be licensed as a title insurance agent. Unless the Agent is also licensed as a title insurance agent, he or she should not take possession of the check.

*3*

# Carrying Out the Signing

## IDENTIFYING BORROWERS

**If a borrower's driver license contains a last name suffix ("Jr." or "II") but the loan documents do not contain the suffix, does the "Less But Not More" rule apply?**

Since an ID card is presented by a document signer as the authoritative and controlling standard the Notary Signing Agent must use for ascertaining the identity of a signer the Agent does not personally know, the "Less But Not More" rule dictates that the typed name in which a borrower must sign cannot be greater than the name appearing on the ID. The name on the document must be "less but not more" than the name appearing on the borrower's ID card.

However, the "Less But Not More" rule should only be used with *middle* names. When a borrower identifies himself with an ID card that contains a last name suffix, the Notary Signing Agent should ensure that the loan documents contain the suffix. It would be unwise for the Agent to proceed with the signing of documents without it.

**Can I positively identify a borrower who presents an ID card with the name Scott J. Smith but the documents require him to sign in the name "J. Scott Smith"?**

Many states define satisfactory evidence of identity as "the absence of any information, evidence, or other circumstances which would lead a reasonable person to believe that the person whose signature is to be notarized is not the person he or she claims to be." (Fla. Stat. 117.05[5][b]) In this instance, a Notary Signing Agent could reasonably conclude that "Scott J. Smith" and "J. Scott Smith" are not the same person.

This is no small point. The order in which the names appear on an ID card matters, even if all other information on the ID matches the individual. Today, identity thieves can manufacture replicas of state-issued driver's licenses that resemble genuine IDs in every respect, right down to the photograph and physical description.

In real property transactions, the stakes are even higher. In our mobile society, where business transactions between strangers are the rule rather than the exception, we rely heavily upon the Notary Public to verify that the signers of important documents are who they claim to be. This is why county recorders and lenders require deeds and loan documents to bear the certification of a Notary Public who has verified the identity of the signing property owner. The Notary Signing Agent is a guardian of the property rights of individuals and businesses.

At a loan signing appointment, some borrowers may become impatient with Agents who resolutely adhere to high identification standards. However, were the Agent to defeat a con artist attempting to defraud the very same homeowner of his property, the Agent would be praised for his diligence, outstanding character, and faithfulness to duty.

### Is there an easy way to identify borrowers with hyphenated names?

Hyphenated names present a challenge to Notaries. Making a positive identification is never "easy" in these cases — especially at the signing table when all parties believe the major selling and negotiating points have been adequately dealt with and are not expecting there to be problems.

The most important principle to keep in mind is that a hyphenated name is essentially *one* name. A borrower whose ID card reads "Roberta Williams-Hill" must sign documents in this name and all documents containing the borrower's typed name must have the full hyphenated name. If the documents omit on part of the hyphenated name, a Notary signing agent could reasonably doubt the two are one and the same person.

Admittedly, the use hyphenated name is on the most difficult issues Notary Signing Agents face. The options for handling this situation are:

1. Determine if the lender or title company would allow the borrower to amend the typed name appearing on all documents by inserting the missing part of the hyphenated name and initialing the addition.

2. Check to see whether the borrower can sign with an "AKA" (Also Known As") signature. With an AKA signature procedure, the borrower signs the full hyphenated name appearing on the ID card followed by the name typed on the documents. For example, "Roberta williams-Hill AKA Roberta Williams."

3. If the Notary Signing Agent is commissioned in a state that allows Notaries to identify document signers with credible witnesses, the borrower can summon witnesses who can identify the borrower in the name printed on the documents.

If these solutions do not solve the problem, the Notary Signing Agent may have to halt the singing until the discrepancy can be resolved.

**I had a signing where the borrower's married name was typed on the documents, but her ID card was issued in her maiden name. The borrower showed me her marriage certificate to prove she had changed names. Was the marriage certificate sufficient proof of her new name?**

If you live in a state with very a specific definition of "satisfactory evidence of identity" that authorizes Notaries to accept certain state-approved IDs and no others (California, for example), or your state defines satisfactory evidence in such a way to disqualify a marriage certificate as a form of identification, then you could not accept the marriage license as proof of a legal name change.

You will need to check your state's Notary laws carefully on this point.

However, even if you live in a state without a clear definition of satisfactory evidence, it is unwise to rely upon a marriage license as a form of identification. At best, a marriage license only indicates that two persons were married on a given date. A marriage license does not contain identifying information that could be used to make a positive identification.

A favorite ruse of identity thieves is to obtain a vital record such as a birth, marriage, or death certificate and steal or construct an identity on the basis of these documents.

The NNA strongly discourages Notary Signing Agents from accepting a marriage license as reliable identification. You may have other options for identifying the borrower, including the use of credible witnesses.

### Does the "Less But Not More" rule apply even when a "Signature Affidavit" is included in the loan document package?

The presence of a "Signature Affidavit" in the documentation is for the benefit of the lender, not the Notary Signing Agent. It is signed to verify that the borrower is known by the other names listed in the Affidavit. These additional names often appear in credit reports and title searches and must be verified to ensure uniformity in the documentation. The borrower must affix his or her official signature for each additional name listed in the affidavit.

Often a "Signature Affidavit" will contain an additional "one and the same" clause, where the borrower must vouch under oath or affirmation that the borrower is the same person as the person listed in the form.

Even though a "Signature Affidavit" is included in the package of loan documents, you still must ensure that the signer's name on the document you are notarizing is equal to or "less but not more" than the name appearing on the signer's identification card. You must always base your identification of a signer on the identification card presented as satisfactory evidence, not the signer's sworn word in a "Signature Affidavit."

For example, if Mary Ann Smith is signing a "Warranty Deed" in her full name but her U.S. Passport contains the shortened name "Mary A. Smith," the fact that a "Signature Affidavit" lists Mary's full name as "Mary Ann Smith" cannot prove she actually bears this name.

## Do I print the borrower's name in the acknowledgment certificate exactly as the name appears in the document or as it appears on the ID card the borrower presents as identification?

County recorders and registers of deeds may reject a document for recording if all names in the document do not match. Therefore, a Notary Signing Agent should print a borrower's name exactly as it appears in the document itself, not on the ID card.

For example, a person's name will appear in three places in a security instrument: in the vesting to indicate how the person is taking title, on the *signature page* directly below the line where the person signs, and in the *Notary's acknowledgment*. Recording officials will check to ensure the names in these three places match.

While all names must match within the security instrument, the names in the document and ID card do not have to match as long as the Notary can make a positive identification. For example, a borrower identified by you as Jane Lee Jones may take title as Jane L. Jones. You may print the name Jane L. Jones in the acknowledgment wording even if the identification card contains the name Jane Lee Jones.

## COMPLETING THE JOURNAL ENTRY

### Can I save time at a signing appointment by completing the journal entry when I get back to my home or office?

The journal entry should be viewed as an essential part of a notarial act that must be completed in the presence of the document signer.

Furthermore, by design a real property transaction is a public act. The security instrument and any conveyance deeds associated with the transaction are executed and notarized before a Notary Public, an official impartial witness, and later filed in the local land records to give the public notice of execution. Additionally, law in many states considers the Notary's journal entry a public record itself. It only makes sense that the journal record of a real property transaction be completed openly before the transacting parties.

From a practical standpoint, there are several additional reasons why the journal entry must be completed at the signing appointment.

1. The document signer has a right to view the full entry requiring the signer's signature (and thumbprint, if required).

2. It is indefensible to ask a borrower to sign an incomplete entry. It is akin to asking the borrower to sign a blank check.

3. By asking the borrower "to just sign my journal and I'll fill in the details later," a Notary Signing Agent sends the wrong message about the importance of a Notary's role as an official witness in a real property transaction.

4. Despite best intentions, a Notary Signing Agent may forget to complete the entry later or may be distracted by other pressing concerns that could cause the Agent to forget important details of the transaction.

A better solution — if you have possession of the loan documents prior to the signing — is to prepare the entries *in advance*, enter the identifying information from the borrower's ID card at the appointment and then have the borrower sign the journal. However, even with this solution there is a potential downside: if the signing is postponed or canceled, you will have several partial entries in your journal for notarizations that were not actually performed.

**Can I simply list the titles of all documents notarized for a loan signing in one line of the journal or write "Loan Documents" in the column marked "Document Kind or Type" to save time and conserve space?**

Some states are very clear that certain information must be entered in the journal for each notarial act the Notary performs. While the desire to save time and conserve space is certainly understandable, it cannot be at the expense of a true, full and accurate record of the notarization.

Each document notarized in connection with a loan signing should contain its own dedicated line entry. Except for Notary Signing Agents in Hawaii, who must complete journal entries "at length" for each act, use of common shortcuts such as ditto marks and a single diagonal line drawn through the signature space for all documents related to a single signer, is an acceptable alternative that will save time.

It is easy to forget at a loan signing where you must make 5 to 6 entries for each signer that the reason you keep a journal is to preserve as a public record written evidence of the performance of a notarial act. Sure, lumping all documents for a single loan signing into one journal entry would conserve space and time, but it would not preserve an easily understandable record that document signers, employers, the public, county clerks, Notary regulating officials, attorneys and the courts could use if there was need to know more specific information about a transaction that occurred months and even years before.

Do not forget that some day you may need the evidence in your journal to testify in court or even counter a frivolous allegation of Notary misconduct. At that time, you will need *all* of the pertinent information from the transaction at your disposal, since you will have long forgotten the details of the transaction under scrutiny.

You should create journal entries with the following maxim in mind: record entries clearly and plainly so any reasonable person could quickly access and understand the specific information requested.

### Which date — the date preprinted on the document or the actual date of signing — is to be entered into the "Document Date" column in the journal?

The plethora of possible document dates on the notarized loan documents can make Notary Signing Agents dizzy. Among the possibilities are:

1. A single preprinted document drafting date.

2. A single signing date (typically added by the signer).

3. An effective date occurring in the past. (For example, just above the place where the borrower signs, there may be the line, "DATED effective this 19th day of June, 2005.") The date of the loan signing appointment might be June 20, 2005.

4. A single future effective date.

5. No document date, except the date of notarization (added by the Notary Signing Agent).

Some documents may have more than one of the above dates.

So, which of these dates is the real "Document Date" to enter into the appropriate column in the journal? The best practices to apply for recording document dates in the journal are:

1. In all cases where there is a preprinted document drafting date, enter this date in the column. This would apply when there is a single preprinted document date and when the document contains a document drafting and actual signing date. The document drafting date typically will be found at the top of the document.

2. In cases where there is only a single signing date (whether preprinted or added by the borrower), enter this date in the column.

3. If the document has neither a drafting nor signing date, write "No Date" in the column. For example, many affidavits do not contain a document drafting date or a space for the signer to add a signing date next to his or her signature. The date added by the Agent to the jurat wording will be noted as the date of notarization in the applicable journal column. In this case, there is no document date.

4. In circumstances where there is mention of a single future or effective date occurring in the past, record this date in the "Document Date" column with a notation underneath (e.g., "Future effective date").

Always remember that the journal entry serves an important evidentiary purpose. If you were presented with a document in court and asked if this was the document you notarized on a particular date, the information you record in the "Document Date" column could help you remember the transaction or rule out the possibility that you notarized it (because the document had a different date than the date you noted).

**What should a Notary Signing Agent do if after journal entries have been completed, the borrower halts the signing before signing the documents?**

The Agent should make a notation in the "Additional Comments" column of the journal that the notarization for the entry was not completed and give a brief explanation. If necessary, use the unused spaces in any additional entries to record these notes.

Entries in the journal should not be altered or lined out, because they may provide valuable evidence later on if the halted signing was the result of impropriety or fraud.

## WHAT TO DO IF?

### How long should I wait for a borrower to show up at the signing location?

Occasionally, a Notary Signing Agent will arrive for an appointment to find the borrower is not home.

Just how long you should wait for the borrower to arrive is often spelled out in the contract for services you signed with the assigning company. Many signing services will require Agents to wait 30 minutes before they will be compensated for a "no show" appointment. Some companies compensate partially for missed appointments, while others will compensate only if the Agent has confirmed the appointment with the borrower the day or night before.

It is a good rule of thumb to attempt to reach the borrower if the borrower is 15 minutes late. If the borrower is 30 minutes late, you should leave a message with the borrower to acknowledge the missed appointment.

As soon as possible contact the assigning agency to inform them of the "no show" and inquire regarding the disposition of documents.

### Who should call the lender for an explanation of loan terms or to ask questions — the Notary Signing Agent or the borrower?

Usually the borrower should call the lender to discuss any loan matters. The Notary Signing Agent should only call the lender if directed by the contracting company. Adding a Notary to the discussion can only complicate matters, and is not appropriate, because the business of the loan is really between the borrower and lender. It may also lead to accusations of the unauthorized practice of law by the Notary.

There is an exception to this standard rule — if the question or clarification pertains directly to the Notary Signing Agent's task or role. For example, if a borrower wants to make a correction on any of the documents — especially on a document that must be notarized and recorded — the Notary should be involved in the conversation. The lender may have a policy not to permit corrections, in which case the lender will need to direct the Notary how to proceed.

## What should the Notary Signing Agent do if a borrower does not have certain information at hand to properly complete the "Statement of Information" form?

The "Statement of Information" is the most labor-intensive document for the borrower to complete in the entire set of loan documents. The form asks borrowers to list previous employers and residences in the past 10 years and provide the names of ex-spouses and other family information. If the borrower has held several different jobs or moved frequently, it can take some time to complete the form.

For this reason, title companies often mail or fax the form directly to the borrower in advance of the loan signing appointment so that the borrower can have sufficient time to fill out the form.

Upon receiving the loan documents the morning of a signing appointment, astute Notary Signing Agents often fax the form to the borrower hours before the scheduled appointment time so it can be completed before the Agent arrives.

Of course, there are instances when the document package is shipped directly to the borrower and the Notary Signing Agent will not know if the "Statement of Information" is included in the package. You can ask the borrower to find this form and to complete it before you arrive.

If the form must be completed at the time of the appointment and the borrower lacks certain information, the Notary Signing Agent usually can leave the form with the borrower to complete. The Agent should instruct the borrower to fax the completed copy to the title company the next day in advance of mailing the original.

## Are there any special procedures that a Notary Signing Agent should keep in mind when the borrower signs with an illegible signature?

You should not be concerned with this as long as the chosen signature is the way the borrower normally signs his or her name. However, Agents must be satisfied that an illegible signature is the borrower's true signature.

Mortgage fraud and identity theft are becoming more prevalent. The FBI recently noted that 5 to 10 percent of all mortgage loan applications contain some form of fraud or misrepresentation.

Notary Signing Agents must be keenly aware that the borrower signing closing documents may not be the person he or she purports to be and be ever vigilant to spot a forgery in the making. It is inevitable that some frauds will not be detected in the loan approval process and will progress toward closing.

To be sure, an impostor or identity thief can use a completely legible signature to commit a forgery. Whether legible or illegible, you can spot forgeries in the making by applying the following fraud-deterrent tips:

1. Make a positive identification prior to signing documents. Check the ID card's features and security enhancements. Look for alterations or signs of tampering. Match the physical description on the ID with the signer appearing in front of you.

2. Keep a journal and obtain a journal signature. Impostors who are asked to sign a Notary journal entry may be reluctant to do so or it may actually deter them from carrying out their crime. If you can get a thumbprint in the journal, all the better.

3. Compare signatures. With a signed journal entry and the borrower's ID in hand, examine both signatures. They don't have to be exact, but they should be *reasonably similar*. If the signatures are starkly different, ask the signer if he or she has recently changed the manner of signing.

4. Be observant as documents are signed. Does the borrower vary the signature from page to page? Does the borrower take an unusually long time to sign? Is the borrower in a hurry to sign? These signals could indicate a possible crime in the making.

## What is the procedure for correcting an incorrect date typed on the "Right to Cancel" (RTC) form?

Often a Notary Signing Agent will be handed an assignment with documents bearing a date in the past. In most cases, this is because the original signing appointment was rescheduled.

If the date on the RTC is incorrect, then the Notary Signing Agent should instruct the borrower to line out the incorrect date, insert the correct date above or to the side and initial the correction. The National Notary Association recommends that Agents not make the corrections themselves, although most lenders allow Agents to do so.

## Should I direct a borrower to initial the dates on a "Notice of Right to Cancel" form when no changes or corrections have been made to the document?

It is a widespread practice for a signer of a legal document to initial any corrections made to the text of a document. In a loan signing context, the same procedure generally applies. When dates entered into a "Notice of Right to Cancel" document are incorrect, these dates must be corrected and properly initialed by the borrower.

However, the question here is whether such initials are necessary when the dates are correct, and whether their presence in such cases is harmful or detrimental.

Unless a lender specifically directs, when the dates on a "Notice of Right to Cancel" form are correct as typed or are entered at the time of the signing, a Notary Signing Agent should not direct a borrower to initial these dates.

Notary Signing Agents have informed the NNA that some lenders will not fund a loan if the "Notice of Right to Cancel" form contains such "needless" initials without the "Notice of Right to Cancel" form being redrawn and signed by the borrower, and after a new 3-day rescission period expires.

In addition to signing the "Notice of Right to Cancel" document, some lenders require a borrower to initial the dates on the form even when the dates are correct to acknowledge awareness of the rescission period in force. One lender even requires the "Notice of Right to Cancel" instrument to be initialed, and not signed, by the borrower.

Notwithstanding the varieties of practice, a Notary Signing Agent should not conclude that since one lender requires initials all lenders must, or that it is desirable to obtain initials as an extra precaution (as for example, when the Notary Signing Agent writes in the dates on the form).

A lender usually adds a special "initial here" stamp near the rescission period dates on the "Notice of Right to Cancel" to indicate that borrower initials are required.

### If a federal holiday falls on a weekend, does the day the holiday is observed count as a business day for the purposes of calculating the rescission period?

The Truth in Lending Act (TILA) specifies that borrowers of qualifying loans are entitled to a 3-day "cooling off" period before the transaction becomes final. The rescission period begins on the next business day following execution of loan papers and ends at midnight on the third business day. A "business day" is any day of the week except Sunday and 10 holidays specified in 5 U.S.C. Sec. 6103(a).

On rare occasions a holiday will fall on a weekend and banks, the post office and government offices will be closed the following Monday in observance of the holiday. Or it might fall on Saturday, with many private offices closing to observe the holiday on Friday, the day before.

In 5 U.S.C. 6103(a), 4 of the 10 federal holidays listed are date-specific: New Year's Day — January 1; Independence Day — July 4; Veterans Day — November 11; and Christmas Day — December 25. The other six holidays affected in rescission period calculations do not have a specific date assigned. For example, the birthday of Martin Luther King, Jr., is observed on the third Monday in January and Columbus Day, the second Monday in October.

In the commentary on the TILA, the Federal Reserve Board provides an important official interpretation of the term "business day" in relation to these 4 date-specific holidays. According to the commentary, the only date that counts when computing the rescission period is the date of the actual holiday itself. In the case of Independence Day falling on a Sunday, the Monday following would count as a business day for rescission period calculations — even though the holiday was nationally observed on Monday, with government office closures, etc.

Notary Signing Agents can no longer assume that if banks, the post office and other state and federal government offices are closed on a weekday in observance of a holiday falling on a weekend, the day of observance would not count as one of the three business days.

### In cases where document dates appear in the past, should I have the borrower correct the dates?

The answer to this question depends upon the lender's instructions. A Notary Signing Agent should never change document dates or instruct a borrower to do so unless the lender approves. In many instances corrections made to the Deed of Trust or Mortgage and promissory note will automatically result in the need to redraw the documents. Therefore, it is always best to obtain directions before any corrections are made.

Agents will discover that a wide variety of practices exist among lenders. Some lenders will require the documents to be corrected to reflect the current date. In this case, the standard rules with respect to correcting documents apply — the borrower should cross out the old date, write in the current date, and initial the corrections.

Other lenders will allow the pre-printed dates to be left unchanged and instruct the Notary Signing Agent to have the borrowers enter the actual date of signing into any date lines calling for a date. These date lines typically appear near signature lines at the bottom of documents.

Still other lenders will require the document package to be redrawn with the correct dates and a new appointment scheduled once the new loan package with the correct dates is issued.

There is always one instance when an incorrect date *must* be changed — when a pre-printed date entered into a notarial certificate is not the actual date of notarization. The Notary Signing Agent must correct this date to reflect the date the document was notarized. Lenders and title companies will seldom object to the Agent correcting these dates. However, to be on the safe side, the Agent should always inform the lender of the need to correct dates within the notarial certificates when obtaining instructions with respect to the other documents.

### What are the procedures for conducting a loan signing with an attorney in fact who is signing for an absent borrower?

Occasionally a loan signing will be attended by a person who has been designated as an absent borrower's legal representative or attorney in fact to sign loan papers for the borrower. Attorney in fact loan signings require certain adjustments to the typical procedures for conducting the signing appointment. These procedures are as follows:

1. Verify signing capacity: A Notary Signing Agent should ask to see the original or a certified copy of the power of attorney document naming the person as attorney in fact. The Agent should verify capacity even when it is not a requirement of state law to do so.

2. Check with the lender to determine if any unique signing procedures apply, including the exact form of the signature the attorney in fact must use. A signature such as "John J. Johnson by James J. Johnson, attorney in fact" will be required, but the lender or title company should provide the exact verbiage. Also check to determine the form for adding initials.

3. Determine if any instruments must be notarized with a jurat. While an attorney in fact may make an acknowledgment in a representative capacity, the attorney in fact may not take an oath or affirmation on a "Signature Affidavit" "Occupancy Affidavit," "Mortgagor's Affidavit," or other instrument requiring a jurat. If any of these documents appear in the loan package, contact the lender to see if they can be acknowledged instead or to be given further instruction for how to handle these forms.

4. Ask if a particular acknowledgment form must be used for the attorney in fact signing. Many states prescribe an "attorney in fact acknowledgment certificate" or a more generic "representative acknowledgment" for use by signers executing documents in a representative capacity. This consideration will not apply to Notary Signing Agents in states that use "all-purpose" acknowledgments.

**When an attorney in fact is signing documents for the principal, should I ask to see the original power of attorney document naming the person as attorney in fact?**

The best practice for handling this situation is to verify the attorney in fact's signing capacity, but ultimately the answer to this question depends upon the Notary laws of each particular state. In some states, Notaries must certify in an acknowledgment certificate that the document signer is the designated attorney in fact. Proof of signing capacity would be required.

In other states, Notaries do not have a statutory responsibility to determine a person's representative capacity; instead, the Notary signs an acknowledgment certificate certifying that the person making the acknowledgment executed the document in "his or her authorized capacity." The Notary's only legal responsibility is to make a positive identification of the person.

In cases where an attorney in fact is executing loan documents, lenders often will require an original or certified copy of the power of attorney document to be returned with the signed documents.

### What should I do if my Notary stamp or seal is illegible?

Affix a second stamp or seal impression near the illegible impression if there is room and the second impression of the seal will not obscure any signatures or written text. If there is not sufficient room to add a second seal impression, attach a "loose" notarial certificate containing the same wording as in the preprinted acknowledgment or jurat. Print the words, "See attached certificate" in large letters and properly complete, sign, and affix a legible seal to the loose certificate. Finally, securely staple the loose certificate to the document.

### I have noticed that some documents call for the signature of the "Closing Agent." Do I sign these forms?

It is critically important that the roles of Notary Signing Agent and closing agent not be confused. Closing Agents prepare documents, disburse funds and coordinate the consummation of a real estate transaction. Signing Agents work for closing agents; they are involved only with the signing portion of the closing agent's duties. Signing Agents do not draw up documents, disburse funds or provide abstraction of title. They act mainly as a courier and impartial witness for signings.

It is imperative to remember that the Signing Agent is first and foremost a Notary. It is the Notary Signing Agent's obligation to avoid overstepping any statutory bounds. The Notary Signing Agent should refrain from giving legal advice and should always refer questions to the closing agent or to the lender. Otherwise, the Notary Signing Agent may be held liable for any problems that arise from his or her advice, and face possible prosecution for the unauthorized practice of law.

When you see a signature line for a "Closing Agent," you should not sign. It is likely that you would find such a signature line on the escrow instructions, where the closing agent must certify that he or she closed the loan properly. You can safely assume that the title or escrow officer in charge of closing the transaction will add his or her signature once the documents have been signed by the borrower and notarized by you.

### What should I tell a borrower who asks how his or her credit score was calculated?

The credit report contains an individual's credit history and current credit standing, including late payments, defaults and bankruptcies.

A credit file contains five types of information.

1. Identification information, including the person's name, verification of social insurance numbers and date of birth, place of residence, previous residence, marital status, place of employment, and previous places of employment.

2. Credit information: Credit accounts include loans and accounts with banks.

3. Retailers, credit card issuers, and other lenders: The types of accounts, monthly payment amounts, manner of payments, current balances, and amounts past due will be noted.

4. Public record information: Any information contained in court records (collections, judgments, bankruptcies, secured loans, etc.).

5. Inquiries: Inquiries show credit grantors when the consumer had applied for new credit which could result in additional debt.

"FICO scores" — named after the Fair Isaac Corporation (FICO) that developed software for computing credit scores — are used by Equifax, Experian and TransUnion, the three major credit reporting agencies. The higher the FICO score, the lower the individual's credit risk.

Each of the three credit reporting agencies use different names for the "FICO" score, although each uses the same methodology for calculating the scores. The names are as follows:

1. BEACON® (Equifax)

2. Experian/Fair Isaac Risk Model (Experian)

3. EMPIRICA® (TransUnion)

Virtually every loan package will contain a disclosure form informing the borrower that the borrower has a right to receive a copy of the credit file used to approve the loan, and provide an address where the borrower can write to obtain the report. In addition, some lenders provide a copy of the actual credit scores in the documentation.

**I have noticed there are times when the check boxes on the "Impound Authorization" are not checked. What should I do in cases like these?**

The "Impound Authorization" is a document in which the borrower authorizes the lender to collect and manage that portion of a borrower's monthly payments for taxes, insurances (hazard and mortgage insurance, if required) and other items as they become due.

In cases where establishment of an impound account is a requirement for obtaining the loan, a check box for authorizing creation of the account will be checked. An impound account is typically required in purchase transactions where the borrower's down payment is less than 20 percent. In refinance transactions, policies vary depending upon the amount of equity the borrower has in the property.

If an impound account is not required and the borrower has not informed the lender in advance of the signing appointment whether he or she prefers to set up an account, the "Impound Authorization" will appear with blank check boxes.

Following is the text of one such "Impound Authorization":

"This loan does not require the establishment of an Impound Account as a condition of the loan, however:

☐ I/we nevertheless want the Lender to establish an Impound Account for the following items:

☐ Hazard Insurance (fire only) It is my/our responsibility to pay for any mid-year premium increases which have resulted from changes to my/our insurance policy or from changing insurance companies.

☐ Real Estate Property Taxes

☐ I/we do not want the Lender to establish an Impound Account. I/we agree to make timely payments to the appropriate parties for all payment of taxes, insurance premiums, assessments, or other items relating to the Property. If any of these payments become delinquent, I/we agree that the Lender may add impounds for the remainder of the loan term."

As the wording above indicates, a borrower can elect to set up an impound account even when one is not required, and many borrowers choose to do so. Notary Signing Agents should ask the borrower to read the document and mark the check box(es) that represent the borrower's choice, and then sign and date the form.

However, Agents should not explain the document to the borrower.

The "Initial Escrow Account Disclosure," an accompanying form, outlines the activity in an escrow or impound account over the 12 month period beginning with the month the first loan payment is due. In cases where the borrower has asked the lender in advance of the signing to establish an impound account, this form will itemize the amounts to be impounded each month, and the amounts and dates disbursements will be made for the impounded items. If the borrower has informed the lender he or she does not want an escrow account, the form will likely contain zero amounts and a zero balance.

**If a loan package contains separate IRS Forms 4506 for a husband and wife to sign, is it necessary to have them also sign each other's form?**

IRS Form 4506 contains a signature line for the spouse of the signer since the IRS needs the spouse's consent to release tax returns if the couple files taxes jointly. In cases where both marriage partners are borrowers, loan document packages will often contain a separate form for each borrower to sign. It is not necessary to have each partner sign the other partner's form, but there is no harm having partners sign either.

However, if both partners are borrowers on the loan and the package contains only one Form 4506, then it will be necessary to have the primary borrower sign first, followed by the co-borrower underneath. If the form contains additional instruction pages with initials appearing at the bottom, make sure that both borrowers initial these pages.

**If a borrower will not sign a "Compliance Agreement" or a "Correction Agreement: Limited Power of Attorney," should I continue with the signing?**

On occasion, a borrower may object to signing a particular document. The two documents mentioned deal with how typographical errors and minor mistakes in the documentation will be corrected. By signing the "Compliance Agreement," the borrower pledges to assist in correcting these errors, while by executing the "Correction Agreement: Limited Power of

Attorney" the borrower appoints an agent to make corrections for the borrower. Both forms are routinely notarized.

Since timely correction of errors in the documents is an important prerequisite for selling the loan to a potential investor in the secondary mortgage market, the importance of signing these two documents cannot be overstated.

A borrower may question whether matters of substance, such as errors in the interest rate, loan term or monthly payment amount constitute "typographical errors" and "misspellings." Of the two documents, borrowers are less resistant to signing the "Compliance Agreement," since the borrower will make the corrections at the lender's request. They may be less willing to appoint an agent to perform this task for them, although most powers of attorney documents of this nature contain a statement that the lender will furnish the borrower with copies of all corrected documents.

If a lender or title agent can be reached during the signing, the first step is to have the representative field the borrower's concerns and attempt to resolve the difficulty.

If the lender or title company cannot be reached, the best course of action is to attach a "sticky note" to the unsigned document stating the reason why the borrower would not sign. The Agent should sign or initial the "Note" and then proceed to have the borrower execute the remaining documents.

Finally, at the conclusion of the signing or the next business day, the Notary Signing Agent should inform the assigning company of the fact. This will give the lender or title company time to take the matter up with the borrower and execute any needed documents before the closing.

**How should I handle a borrower who insists on reading the documents word for word, especially when I might miss or be late for another scheduled appointment?**

There are a number of ways to handle this situation, but first you should realize it is the borrower's right to read the documents before signing them. If an Agent pressures a borrower to sign the documents within a certain period of time, the borrower could become upset and even irate, and possibly call off the signing.

However, the following strategies can help manage this eventuality with a minimum of conflict:

1. Make sure to allow sufficient time between appointments, including a built-in "buffer" to compensate for signings that run late. Remember to factor in time for travel between locations and any possible delays due to inclement weather, traffic, etc. Do not allow your poor planning or over-scheduling to be the reason for appointments running late.

2. Before you begin, let the borrower know how long the appointment should take and what your time constraints are. At the close of the month and with date-sensitive transactions, the consequences for running late could be serious. You may have to tell the borrower that another client is depending upon you to arrive in a timely manner to handle their signing.

3. If the transaction has a rescission option, execute the "Notice of Right to Cancel" first or early on in the signing. This way, you can remind the borrower that he has 3 business days to review the documents before the transaction can close. However, if the loan does not contain a rescission option, you must honor the borrower's wishes to proceed with the signing at the borrower's own pace.

4. It is also a good idea to execute the "Note," security instrument and settlement statement early on in the appointment, since these documents typically are scrutinized more carefully than the others.

5. If you run the risk of missing your next scheduled appointment, attempt to call the borrower, explain that your current appointment is taking longer than expected and ask if the borrower's schedule is flexible. Before

considering whether to cut an appointment short prior to finishing, attempt to contact the lender's agent or title company contact to inform them of the situation. You may be able to negotiate a solution, such as having the borrower return the signed documents or setting up a return appointment.

## What are the steps I should take if a borrower unexpectedly halts a signing?

First and foremost, be professional. Remain calm and composed. Do not argue with or attempt to dissuade the borrower. Even if it means you will not be paid for the signing, always remember the borrower calls the shots. It's the borrower's transaction, not yours.

Second, collect all signed and unsigned documents — including the borrower's copies — and take them with you. Never leave these documents with the borrower.

Third, inform the borrower that you will contact all parties involved in the transaction. Ask the borrower if there is anything he or she would like you to convey to the lender or title agent.

Finally, contact your assigning company and ask what to do with the documents. In most instances, you will be asked to return the documents. If the documents are unsigned, you may be instructed to wait a couple of days to see if the situation can be resolved and a new signing appointment can be scheduled.

Chapter

4

# Closing Out the Signing

## CHECKING DOCUMENTS

**What are some examples of mistakes that could cause a county recorder or register of deeds to reject a deed of trust or mortgage for recording?**

Second only to submission of an incorrect fee, county recorders report that the failure of Notaries to properly complete acknowledgment certificates is the single greatest reason documents are rejected for recordation. Among the errors most often cited are:

1. Failure to affix the Notary's signature or seal.

2. An illegible Notary signature or seal.

3. An improper form of acknowledgment (*e.g.*, an "individual" certificate is used for a document executed by an attorney in fact").

4. Errors within the Notary's acknowledgment (*e.g.*, omission of a date or name of principal, or misspelled name of principal).

5. Omission of the form of acknowledgment altogether (*i.e.*, the Notary merely "stamps and signs" without completing a certificate).

## Could I be liable if I miss a signature or a notarization?

It might be considered negligence for a Notary Public to notarize a paper without the borrower's signature. In an acknowledgment in which the borrower's signature is evidence that the borrower freely executed the instrument, lack of a signature voids the notarization and the underlying instrument.

It may also be negligence to "miss a notarization," although in using this phraseology, a title, escrow, or loan officer may mean a number of things, including:

1. A failure to complete an acknowledgment or jurat certificate.

2. A failure to enter the correct venue.

3. An incorrect date printed in the notarial certificate.

4. A misspelling of a borrower's name in the notarial certificate.

5. A failure to administer an oath or affirmation as required.

6. A failure to affix the official seal to the document.

7. A failure to sign the certificate in the Notary's full commission name.

8. In some states, a failure to add the Notary's commission information underneath the signature.

Any improper notarization exposes the Notary Signing Agent to liability at the hands of a lender, title company, escrow agency — and even the borrower — if the improper act is the direct or proximate cause of the loss.

For example, an improper notarization might delay a loan from funding and cause the loss of a rate lock, resulting in the borrower incurring a higher interest rate. The borrower might blame the Notary Signing Agent for the increased interest on the loan suffered as a result of the Agent's error.

Take the case of a Notary Signing Agent who forgot to notarize a deed of trust. The Notary's omission was not caught by the title agent, who sent the deed to be recorded. Due to high volume of submissions at the county recorder's office, the county recorder allowed the deed to sit for weeks, and then rejected it for recording because it was not notarized. The Agent's omission cost the lender over $6,000 in lost interest. The lender sought reimbursement of the lost interest from the title company; the title company sought reimbursement from the signing service that hired the Agent; and the signing service entered a claim against the Agent's Notary bond to recover its loss. Ultimately, the Agent had to repay the bonding company.

## SHIPPING DOCUMENTS

### Am I responsible for keeping the tracking number on the loan documents?

You should keep a record of the tracking number for the shipment of loan documents back to the closing agent for at least two reasons:

1. Most lenders, escrow offices and signing services will ask you to include the tracking number for the shipment of the documents to the closing agent in any correspondence you submit to confirm the signing was completed.

2. In the event the package is misplaced or lost in transit, you can produce the tracking number to prove you shipped the package.

Most signing services and closing agents include a shipping envelope and self-addressed air bill with the document package that is shipped to you for the assignment. In many cases, the sender has removed and retained the shipper's copy with the tracking number. Even when this is the case, you should write the tracking number down anyway. Do not assume that the closing agent has the tracking number.

## Will I ever have to pay for the shipment of documents?

Notary Signing Agents should never pay for the return shipment of documents unless the shipment is the result of the Agent's mistake or error.

Usually a pre-addressed shipping envelope and air bill is included in the loan document package with the recipient's account number to prevent the Notary Signing Agent from incurring the costs for the shipment. When return packaging is not included or the account number is not present on the air bill, the Agent should contact the assigning company or closing agent to obtain the account number.

However, if upon inspecting the documents a closing agent discovers the Notary Signing Agent made a mistake that necessitates a return trip to the borrower to re-execute documents, the Agent should pay for the return of the second shipment.

## COLLECTIONS

### What's the best way to keep track of collectables?

Collectables, or "accounts receivable" as they are often called, are fees owed to you for the Notary Signing Agent services you have rendered. Most companies providing Notary Signing Agent assignments are reputable and pay their accounts on time. Regrettably, all too often Agents inform the National Notary Association of companies that have not paid them for their services and ask what they can do to be paid.

The following is a straight forward collections process you can implement in your Notary Signing Agent business.

Immediately following the conclusion of a loan signing assignment, you should invoice the assigning company for the fees you are due. The invoice is your first generation request for payment and should include the following:

1. The invoice date;

2. Invoice number;

3. The customer's address;

4. Your business address;

5. The date services were rendered;

6. The name of the borrower(s);

7. The order number (if applicable);

8. A description of the services rendered and

9. The total amount due.

Many signing services have an alternative billing/payment process. Some issue loan assignment forms that they expect to be return-faxed with details of the signing confirmation or have an online signing confirmation form Agents complete. Some even take signing completion reports by phone. These methods can substitute for submission of a separate invoice, but remember to retain a hard copy.

Your accounts receivable should be "aged" at the end of each month. At the beginning of the month you should issue your second generation request for payment — a "Statement of Account" — to each of your clients with outstanding accounts. The statement should include the following:

1. Statement date;

2. The customer's address;

3. Your business address;

4. The invoice date;

5. The invoice number;

6. A description of the services rendered;

7. The invoice amount;

8. Any payments received;

9. The remaining balance;

10. An aging column with aged amounts (due less than 30 days, due from 31-60 days and overdue by 60 or more days).

11. The total amount due and

12. The message area.

In the "message" area, you should include a statement that reads, "Your account is now _____ days past due. Please remit payment today." You should allow two weeks for payment on the account.

The third generation request for payment is a phone call to the client's bookkeeper or accounts manager. You should inform the individual that you have not received payment for invoice # _____ in the amount of $ _____ and ask when you can expect to be paid. You should allow two weeks following the phone call for payment on the account.

After the two-week period elapses, it is now 60 days since the date you first mailed the original invoice. At this point, issue a demand letter that reads as follows:

*Your Company Logo*

*Your Name*
*Street Address*
*City, State, Zip*
*Today's Date*

*Recipient Name*
*Title*
*Company Name*
*Company Address*
*City, State, Zip*

*Dear Name of Recipient:*

*Did you forget about sending your payment? Your bill of $_____ is now _____ days overdue.*

*Please disregard this notice if payment has already been sent. Otherwise, please remit payment to the address above immediately.*

*A statement of your account activity is attached. Again, please accept our sincere thanks if payment has already been mailed.*

*Sincerely,*
*Your Name*
*Title*
*Enclosure*

Wait one week to ensure delivery and then follow up with a phone call to the bookkeeper stating that you still have not received payment for invoice # _____ in the amount of $ _____ and ask when you can expect to be paid. You should allow one week following the phone call for payment on the account.

After the one-week period elapses, it is now 75 days since the date you first mailed the original invoice. At this point, issue a second demand letter that reads as follows:

*Your Company Logo*
*Your Name*
*Street Address*
*City, State, Zip*
*Today's Date*

*Recipient Name*
*Title*
*Company Name*
*Company Address*
*City, State, Zip*

*Dear Name of Recipient:*

*Your bill of $_____ is now _____ days overdue. The total amount is due now.*

*This is our second request for payment. If you would like to discuss payment arrangements, or if you believe this amount is incorrect, please call xxx-xxx-xxxx.*

*A statement of your account activity is attached for your review. Please accept our sincere thanks if payment has already been mailed.*

*Sincerely,*
*Your Name*
*Title*
*Enclosure*

Wait one week to ensure delivery and then follow up with a phone call to the bookkeeper stating that you still have not received payment for invoice # _____ in the amount of $ _____ and ask when you can expect to be paid. You should allow one week following the phone call for payment on the account.

After the one-week period elapses, it is now 90 days since the date you first mailed the original invoice. At this point, issue a final demand letter that reads as follows:

*Your Company Logo*
*Your Name*
*Street Address*
*City, State, Zip*
*Today's Date*

*Recipient Name*
*Title*
*Company Name*
*Company Address*
*City, State, Zip*

*Dear Name of Recipient:*

*Your bill of $_____ is now _____ days overdue. The total amount is due now.*

*If your payment in full is not received by _____, your account will be turned over to a collection agency.*

*A statement of your account activity is attached for your review. Please accept our sincere thanks if payment has already been mailed.*

*Sincerely,*
*Your Name*
*Title*
*Enclosure*

If payment is not received by the date you specified in your final demand letter, then you might consider looking in a phone book or on the Internet for a collection agency, especially when the amount due is significant. A collection agency will charge a fee — but at this point the account is 90 days past due, and should be considered a loss.

There are three final steps to take before putting the account to rest:

1. Lodge a formal complaint with your local credit bureau;

2. Report the company to the Better Business Bureau; and

3. File copies of invoices and correspondences in a "Bad Debts" folder to access when you prepare your tax return for the tax year. Bad debts can be expensed on IRS Form 1040 Schedule C "Profit or Loss from Business."

## BUSINESS RECORDS AND TAXES

**I recently purchased the Notary Signing Agent Invoices from the NNA's Notary Essentials Catalog. In the bottom area of the invoice there is a column entitled "Order Number." What does this refer to?**

The "Order Number" in the "Notary Signing Agent Services" area is the number assigned to a loan signing assignment from a company for which the Notary Signing Agent provided services. The number may be one of the following:

1. A "confirmation number" or "reference number" (signing service).

2. A "loan number" (lender or broker).

3. An "escrow number" (escrow agency).

The "Order Number" should not be confused with the pre-stamped red "Invoice Number" appearing in the upper right hand corner of the Notary Signing Agent Invoice. The "Invoice Number" identifies the particular invoice you submitted to the assigning company for payment.

### Are my Notary fees exempt from income taxes?

No; it is commonly misunderstood by many Notaries and Notary Signing Agents that fees for notarizations are exempt from income tax. You must report all income earned as a Notary Public or Notary Signing Agent — including the fees charged for notarial acts — on IRS Form 1040 Schedule C. If you have net earnings from self-employment as a Notary Public or Notary Signing Agent, you must pay federal and state (if applicable) income tax on this amount.

However, according to the Instructions for Schedule SE, Notary fees are exempt from *self-employment taxes* as computed by completing IRS Form 1040 Schedule SE.

To claim the exemption of your Notary fees from self-employment tax, you must keep detailed and timely records of the notarizations you perform and the fees charged for these notarizations. While recording notarial acts and fees in an official journal is one place to record Notary fees, many Notary Signing Agents keep a separate log of all loan signings, the notarizations performed in these signings, and the fees they receive.

### Am I required to pay quarterly estimated taxes on my Notary Signing Agent Income?

Estimated tax is the method used to pay tax on income that is not subject to withholding, as is the case when you operate your own business as a Notary Signing Agent.

In most cases, you must make estimated tax payments if you expect to owe at least $1,000 in tax (after subtracting your withholding and credits) and you expect your withholding and credits to be less than the smaller of:

1. 90% of the tax shown on your 2005 tax return; or

2. The tax shown on your 2004 tax return (110% of that amount if you are not a farmer or fisherman and the adjusted gross income shown on that return is more than $150,000 or, if married filing separately for 2005, more than $75,000).

The rationale behind income tax withholding and estimated tax payments is that taxpayers should pay taxes as they earn income regularly throughout the year. Since government operates all throughout the year, it needs to collect its revenues to sustain operations.

Generally, you would make estimated tax payments on a quarterly basis, on the 15th of April, June, September and January of the following year for which tax is due. However, you may elect to pay all of your estimated tax for the year in advance by April 15th, the date when the first quarterly estimated tax payment is due.

If your income is subject to seasonal fluctuations or you receive your income unevenly during the year, you may be able to lower or eliminate the amount of your required estimated tax payment for one or more periods by using the annualized income installment method outlined in IRS Publication 505.

To figure your estimated tax payments, you should obtain IRS Form 1040-ES "Estimated Tax for Individuals." These forms can be found at the IRS Web site at *www.irs.gov.*

### What tax forms do I need to fill out to report income for my Notary Signing Agent business?

In addition to filing IRS Form 1040 "U.S. Individual Tax Return," Notary Signing Agents will need to obtain, complete, and file one or more of the following forms as attachments to Form 1040:

- Form 1040 Schedule C-EZ "Net Profit From Business" or Schedule C "Profit and Loss from Business (Sole Proprietorship)";

- Form 1040 Schedule SE "Self Employment Tax";

- Form 4562 "Depreciation and Amortization" (to claim depreciation on assets placed in service during the previous tax year, to claim amortization that began in the prior year, to make an election under section 179 to expense certain property or to report information on listed property) and

- Form 8829 "Expenses for Business Use of Your Home" (to claim expenses for business use of your home office).

### What is IRS Form 1040 Schedule C?

Schedule C is the main form an individual taxpayer completes to record profit or loss from operating a self-employed business as a sole proprietor. An activity qualifies as a business if your primary purpose for engaging in the activity is for income or profit and you are involved in the activity with continuity and regularity. For example, a sporadic activity or a hobby does not qualify as a business, and income generated from these activities would not be reported on Schedule C.

You must file a Schedule C or C-EZ if you have over $400 of income from your Notary Signing Agent business after expenses.

Schedule C contains the following five parts:

1. <u>Part I: Income</u>. In this section, you would enter your gross receipts from all loan signings during the tax year. After subtracting returns and allowances, and costs of goods sold (Part III), you would arrive at your gross income for the year.

2. <u>Part II: Expenses</u>. In this section, you would list all of the expenses you incurred in operating your business. Lines 8-27 on page 1 of the form are used to categorize your expenses. The amount entered into line 27 ("Other expenses") is derived from Part V of Schedule C on page 2 of Schedule C.

3. <u>Part III: Cost of Goods Sold</u>. Since Notary Signing Agents provide a service and do not typically sell inventoried goods, you may not have to complete this section.

4. <u>Part IV: Information on Your Vehicle</u>. Every Notary Signing Agent will complete this section since using your vehicle in your business is a given. In this section you will summarize the written documentation you have collected and kept during the year. Part IV is completed if you are claiming car or truck expenses on line 9 of Part II of Schedule C and you are not required to file Form 4562 for your business.

5. <u>Part V: Other Expenses</u>. This section is a continuation sheet for expenses that cannot be categorized under Part II. The total amount of all expenses is entered into line 27 on page 1, Part II.

Small businesses with expenses of $5,000 or less may be able to file Schedule C-EZ instead of Schedule C, a short-form version of Schedule C.

## What are common business expenses incurred by Notary Signing Agents?

While you should consult a tax advisor about your specific situation, the following are expenses you may be able to deduct in Part II of IRS Form 1040 Schedule C "Profit or Loss from Business":

1. Expenses incurred for advertising your Notary Signing Agent business.

2. Fees related to the issuance of your Notary commission, including application and filing fees, surety bond premiums, and notarial supplies.

3. Vehicle expenses — utilizing either the IRS standard mileage rate or claiming actual expenses.

4. Training, books, and educational seminars furthering your knowledge as a Notary Signing Agent.

5. Cell phone and cell phone service plans.

6. Computer equipment, fax machine, or photocopier.

7. Computer software.

8. Expense for the use of a home office under certain circumstances.

9. Office supplies.

10. Deductible portion of any travel, meals, or entertainment expense.

## Should I use the standard mileage rate or claim actual expenses on my vehicle?

When you use the standard mileage rate, you multiply the actual miles driven in conducting loan signing assignments and in all business-related trips by the standard mileage rate and enter the amount in Schedule C, Part II, line 9. The per mile rate is adjusted periodically. For example, in 2004, the standard mileage rate was 37.5 cents per mile; in 2005, the amount increased to 40.5 cents per mile.

You should consult a tax advisor to discuss your specific situation. IRS Publication 463 "Travel, Entertainment, Gift, and Car Expenses" states:

> *If you use the standard mileage rate for a year, you cannot deduct your actual car expenses for that year. You cannot deduct the special depreciation allowance (and you do not need to make the election not to claim the allowance), depreciation, or lease payments, maintenance and repairs, gasoline (including gasoline taxes), oil, insurance, and vehicle registration fees.*

> *Choosing the standard mileage rate. If you want to use the standard mileage rate for a car you own, you must choose to use it in the first year the car is available for use in your business. Then in later years, you can choose to use either the standard mileage rate or actual expenses.*

> *If you want to use the standard mileage rate for a car you lease, you must use it for the entire lease period. For leases that began on or before December 31, 1997, the standard mileage rate must be used for the entire portion of the lease period (including renewals) that is after 1997.*

> *If you choose to use the standard mileage rate, you are considered to have chosen not to use the depreciation methods discussed later. This is because the standard mileage rate includes an allowance for depreciation that is not expressed in terms of years. If you change to the actual expenses method in a later year, but before your car is fully depreciated, you have to estimate the remaining useful life of the car and use straight line depreciation.*

The other option for claiming auto expenses on the use of your car for business is to deduct actual expenses such as depreciation, lease payments, registration fees, licenses, gasoline, insurance, repairs, oil, garage rent, tires, tolls and parking fees.

IRS Publication 463 advises that "if you use your car for both business and personal purposes, you must divide your expenses between business and personal use. You can divide your expense based on the miles driven for each purpose."

In addition to expensing the actual costs of running your vehicle, tax rules also state that you can claim a depreciation deduction each year to recover your cost in the car. Rules for claiming a yearly depreciation expense are detailed and strict, so it is best to consult a tax advisor to discuss your specific tax situation.

IRS Publication 463 instructs that "if you deduct actual expenses, include on line 9 the business portion of expenses for gasoline, oil, repairs, insurance, tires, license plates, etc., and show depreciation on line 13 and/or lease payments on line 20a."

**When using the standard mileage rate, do I calculate my mileage expenses using the rate that applied at the time that I completed the travel or the rate that applies when I file my return?**

The question presupposes a circumstance where the rate has increased in intervening years. The IRS adjusts the standard mileage rate occasionally as costs associated with operating a vehicle increase. For 2005, the per-mile rate was increased from 37.5 cents to 40.5 cents.

The important point to remember is that you calculate your mileage expense using the rate in force at the time of travel. For example, the mileage you accrued for business travel in 2004 and that you will expend on your 2004 tax return is subject to the standard mileage rate for 2004 — 37.5 cents per mile. Even though a new higher per-mile rate will be effective at the time you actually filed your 2004 tax return, you may not apply the increased rate to your 2004 business mileage.

However, in figuring your estimated tax payments for 2005, you may use the increased rate to estimate your anticipated mileage expense for the year to more accurately calculate your quarterly estimated tax payments due in April, June, and September, 2005, and in January, 2006.

### What's the best way to keep track of the miles I drive to perform loan signings?

In general, the IRS advises that to claim a business expense, you must keep:

1. Written or documentary records that prove the amount, time, place or destination, and business purpose or relationship. IRS Publication 463 states, "You should keep the proof you need in an account book, diary, statement of expense or similar record. You should also keep documentary evidence that, together with your record, will support each element of an expense."

2. Timely-kept records. You should record the elements of an expense at or near the time of the expense. While ideally you should keep records for travel at the beginning and end of the day of the expense, the IRS advises that it is acceptable to maintain a log on a weekly basis that accounts for business use of your car during the week.

You can purchase log books for recording mileage to and from loan signing appointments at any office supplies store. You can record the mileage in a "Daytimer" or appointment book, or in a personal data assistant (PDA) as well.

### What is IRS Form 1040 Schedule SE?

Schedule SE is completed to figure the tax due on net earnings from self-employment. The Social Security Administration uses the information from Schedule SE to figure your benefits under the Social Security program.

Self-employment tax applies regardless of your age and even if you are already receiving Social Security or Medicare benefits.

You must pay self-employment tax if you have more than $400 in net earnings from self-employment for the tax year.

You determine your net earnings from self-employment by completing Form 1040 Schedule C "Profit or Loss From Business." The profit (or loss) from line 31 is entered into Schedule SE line 2 and is multiplied by .9235. If the resulting amount is greater than $400, self-employment tax must be computed by completing the remainder of the form.

According to the Instructions for Schedule SE, income earned as a Notary Public is exempt from self-employment taxes. The IRS advises in pertinent part:

> 2. *Fees received for services performed as a notary public. If you had no other income subject to SE tax, enter "Exempt-Notary" on Form 1040, line 57. However, if you had other earnings of $400 or more subject to SE tax, enter "Exempt-Notary" and the amount of your net profit as a notary public from Schedule C or Schedule C-EZ on the dotted line to the left of Schedule SE, line 3. Subtract that amount from the total of lines 1 and 2 and enter the result on line 3.*

For the purpose of the exemption, only fees charged for performing notarial acts may be subtracted from net earnings from self-employment; fees for courier and other non-notarial services are not exempt.

## ABOUT THE NNA

The National Notary Association is a professional association of Notaries Public — serving the nation's more than 4.5 million Notaries Public.

As the nation's clearinghouse for information on notarial customs, laws, and practices, the NNA educates its members through regular and special publications, seminars, its annual Conference, and a host of information services.

The Association is perhaps most widely known as the preeminent publisher of literature, videos, and CD-ROMs for and about Notaries and notarization. NNA publications include:

- *The National Notary* magazine
- *Notary Bulletin* newspapers
- *E-zines including* NSA NOW
- *Sorry, No Can Do!* series
- *Notary Basics Made Easy* video instruction program
- *State Notary Law Primers*
- *Preparing For The California Notary Exam*
- *Notary Home Study Course*
- *U.S. Notary Reference Manual*
- *Notary Signing Agent Certification Course*
- *Notary Public Practices & Glossary*
- *Model Notary Acts* of 1984 and 2002

In addition, the NNA is active in legislative advocacy and public affairs and provides Notaries with the highest-quality professional supplies and support services.

Index

# Question Index

# Topic Index

When an attorney in fact is signing documents
for the principal, should I ask to see the original
power of attorney document naming the person
as attorney in fact? . . . . . . . . . . . . . . . . . . . . . . . . . . 69

Should I have the borrower sign the borrower's
copies as well as the originals? . . . . . . . . . . . . . . . . . 44
If a complete set of borrower's copies are not
included in the loan document package, am I
required to make a copy for the borrower? . . . . . . . . 49

## Borrower Questions

Who should call the lender to explain loan terms
or to ask questions – the Notary Signing Agent
or the borrower? . . . . . . . . . . . . . . . . . . . . . . . . . . . . . 62

What should I tell a borrower who asks how
his or her credit score was calculated? . . . . . . . . . . . 71

## Borrower Relations

How long should I wait for a borrower to show
up at the signing location? . . . . . . . . . . . . . . . . . . . . 62
How should I handle a borrower who insists on
reading the documents word for word, especially
when I might miss or be late for another
scheduled appointment? . . . . . . . . . . . . . . . . . . . . . . 75
What are the steps I should take if a borrower
unexpectedly halts a signing? . . . . . . . . . . . . . . . . . . 77

## Compliance Agreement

If a borrower will not sign a "Compliance Agreement"
or a "Correction Agreement: Limited Power of
Attorney," should I continue with the signing? . . . . . 74

## Dates

Which date – the date preprinted on the document or the
actual date of signing – is to be entered into the
"Document Date" column in the journal? . . . . . . . . . 60

## Deed of Trust (Mortgage)

## Deterring Fraud

## Liability

## Loan Types

## Mistakes and Corrections

## Notary Practices

I am a Notary in a state where it is illegal to
notarize an incomplete document. If the legal
description paragraph in a deed of trust or
mortgage says, "See Exhibit A attached hereto

## Notary Seal

## Rescission (Right to Cancel)

## Saving Time

## Taxes

## Title Industry Terms